FLOWERS AND THINGS

Designed by
SETSUKO MITAMURA

Shown on cover. *(3 strands, unless otherwise specified)*

Shown on page 1. *(3 strands, unless otherwise specified)*

Designed by
MISAKO MURAYAMA

Designed by
MISAKO MURAYAMA

Shown on page 4. *(2 strands, unless otherwise specified)*

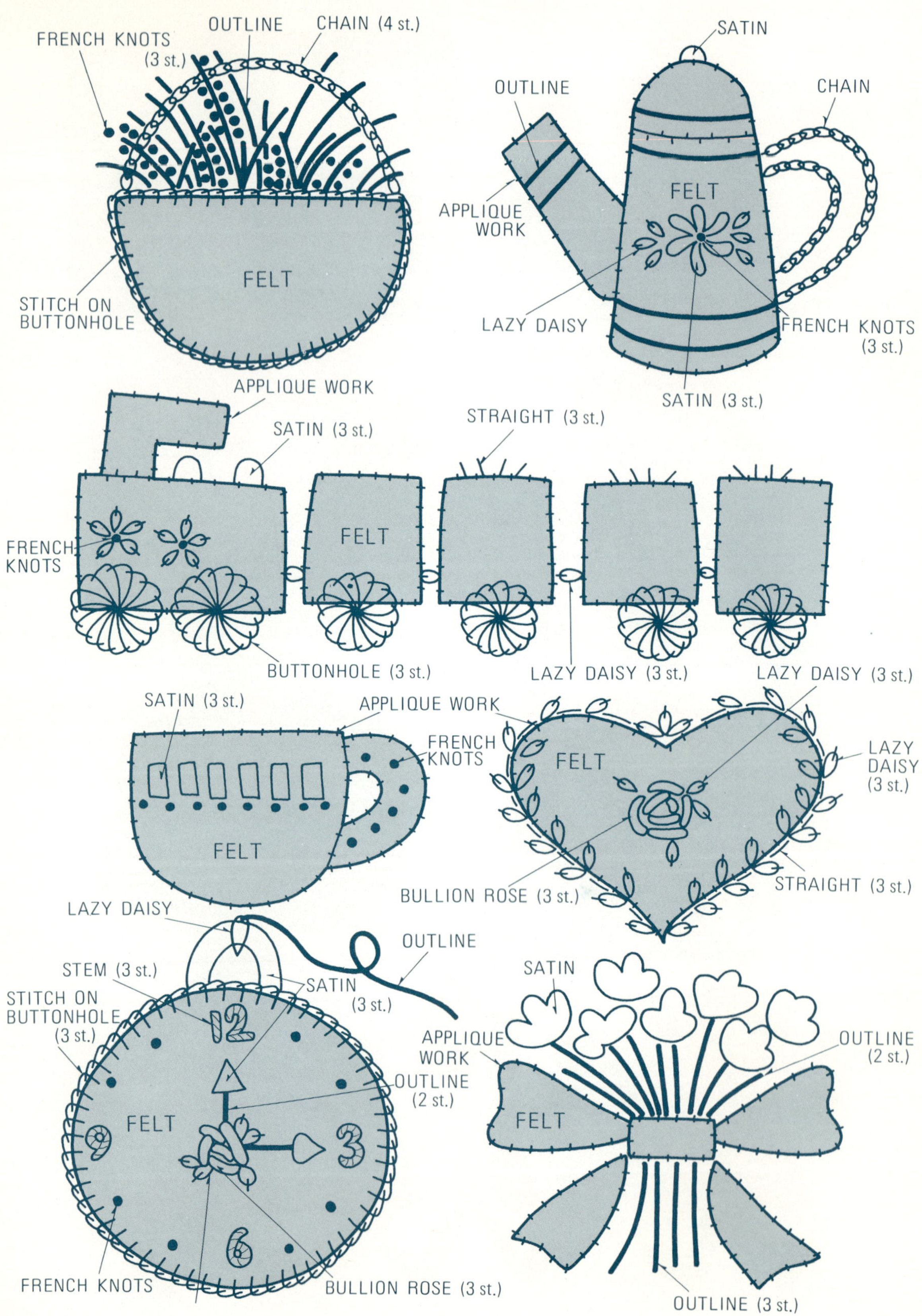

Shown on page 5. *(3 strands, unless otherwise specified)*

Designed by
CHIZU TAKAMIYA

Designed by
CHIZU TAKAMIYA

Shown on page 8. *(3 strands, unless otherwise specified)*

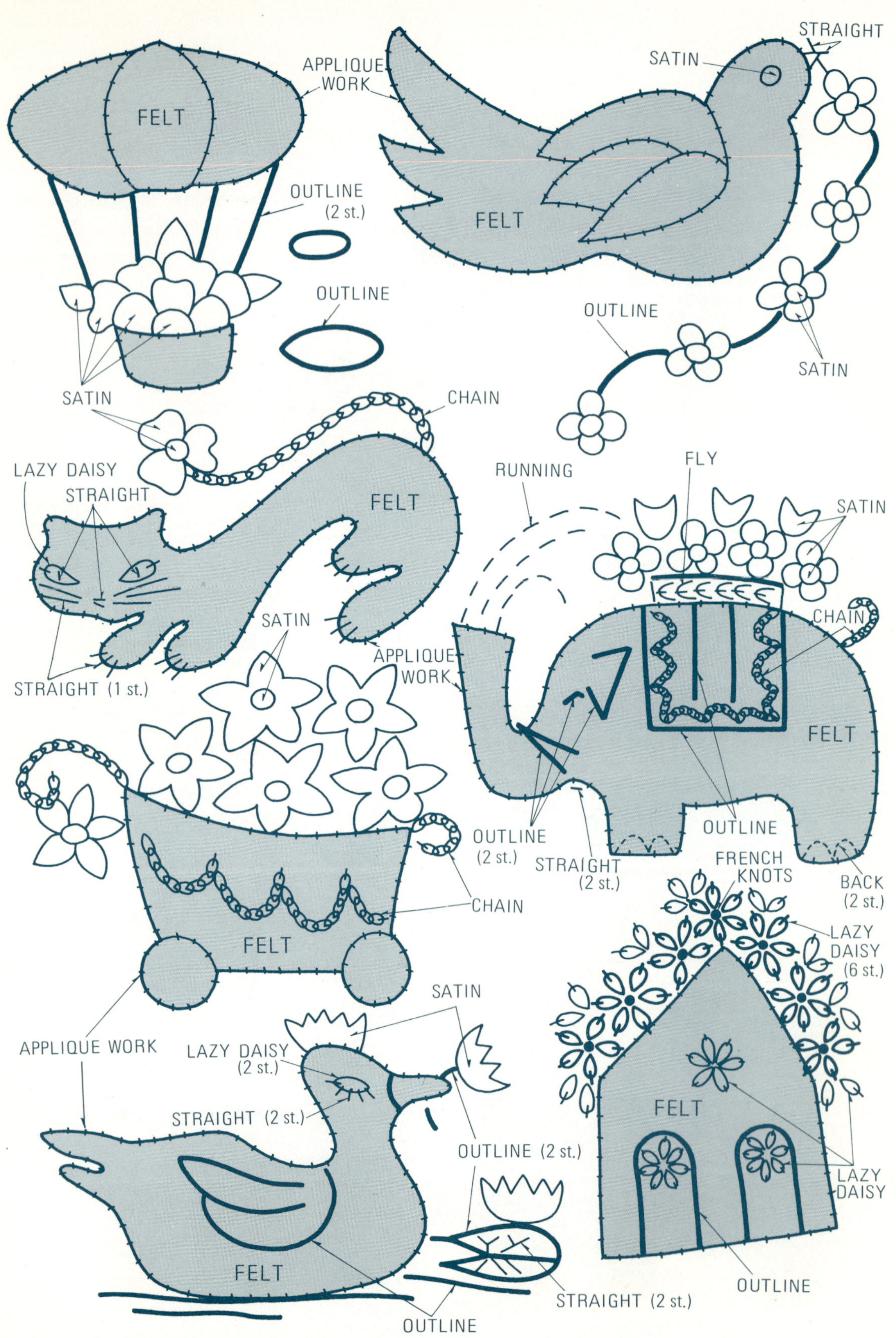

Shown on page 9. *(3 strands, unless otherwise specified)*

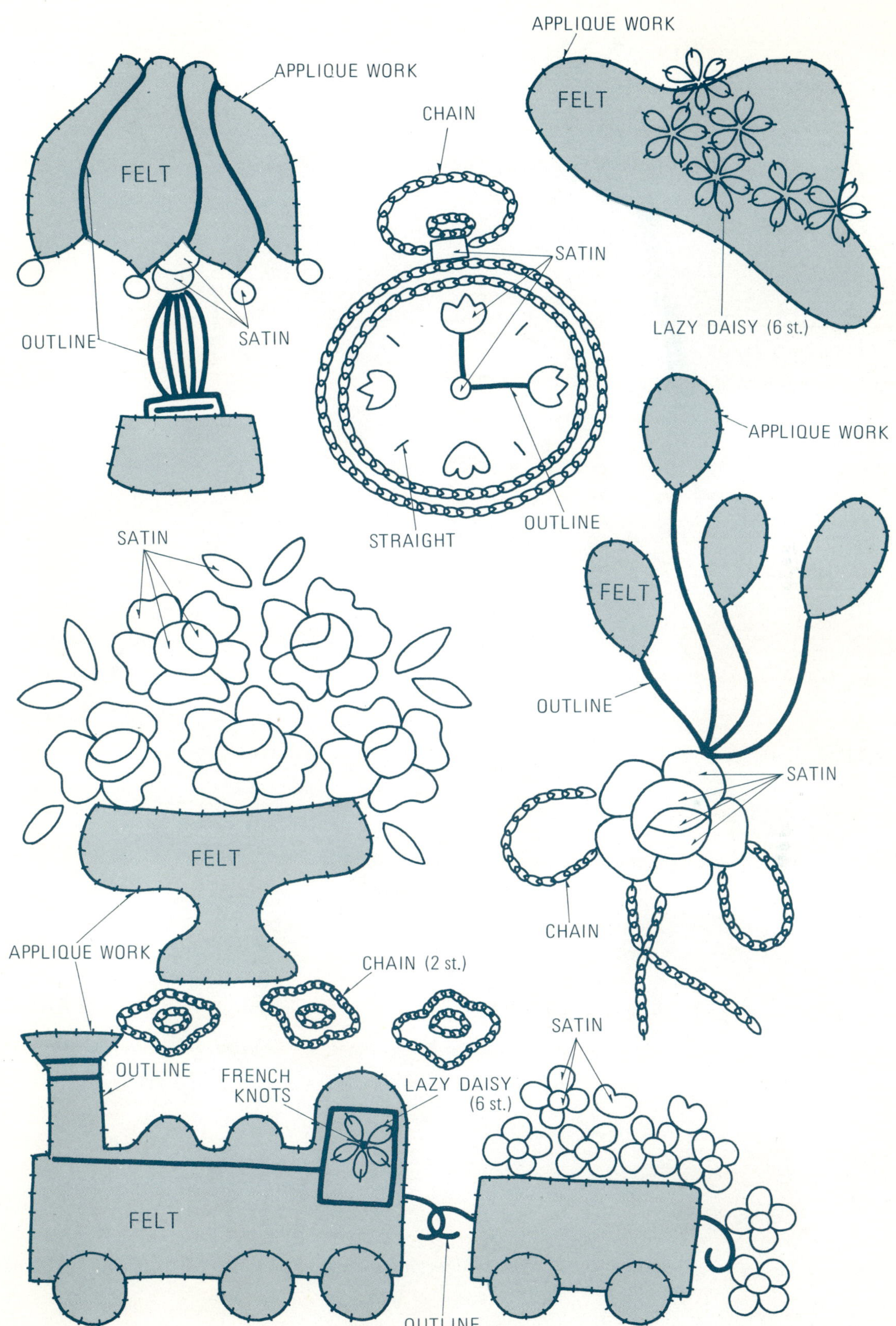

Designed by
TERUMI OTAKA

Designed by
TERUMI OTAKA

Shown on page 12. *(3 strands, unless otherwise specified)*

Shown on page 13. *(3 strands, unless otherwise specified)*

AMUSING ANIMALS

Designed by
MASAKO KIMURA

Designed by
MASAKO KIMURA

Shown on page 16. *(3 strands, unless otherwise specified)*

Shown on page 17. *(3 strands, unless otherwise specified)*

Designed by
KEIKO KASHIWABARA

Designed by
KEIKO KASHIWABARA

Shown on page 20. *(3 strands, unless otherwise specified)*

Shown on page 21. *(3 strands, unless otherwise specified)*

FROM THE TOY CHEST

Designed by
CHIYOKO SAWADA

Designed by
CHIYOKO SAWADA

Shown on page 24. *(2 strands, unless otherwise specified)*

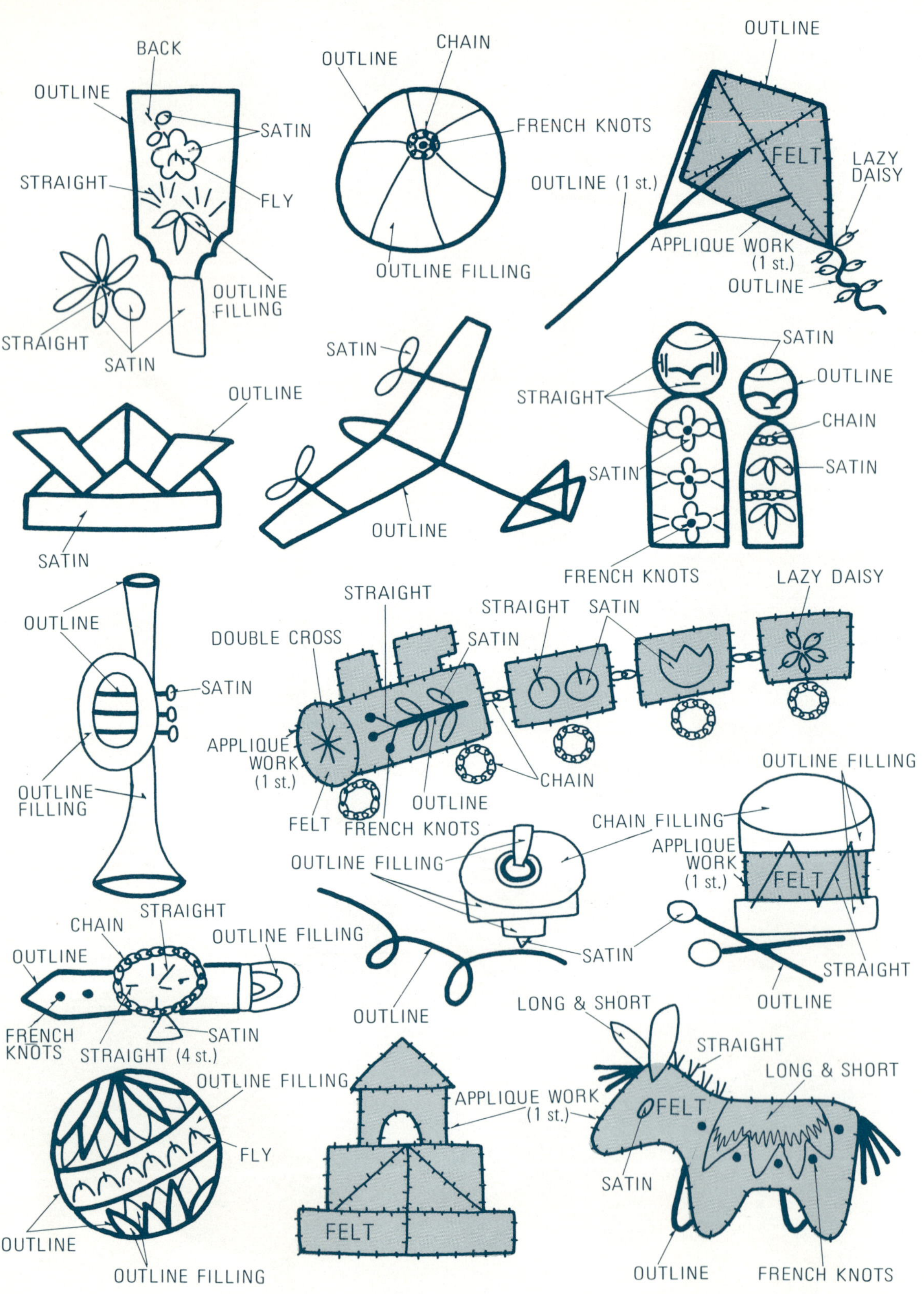

Shown on page 25. *(2 strands, unless otherwise specified)*

Designed by
YOSHIE TAKAMUNE

Designed by
KINUYO WAKAUME

Shown on page 28. *(3 strands, unless otherwise specified)*

Shown on page 29. *(4 strands, unless otherwise specified)*

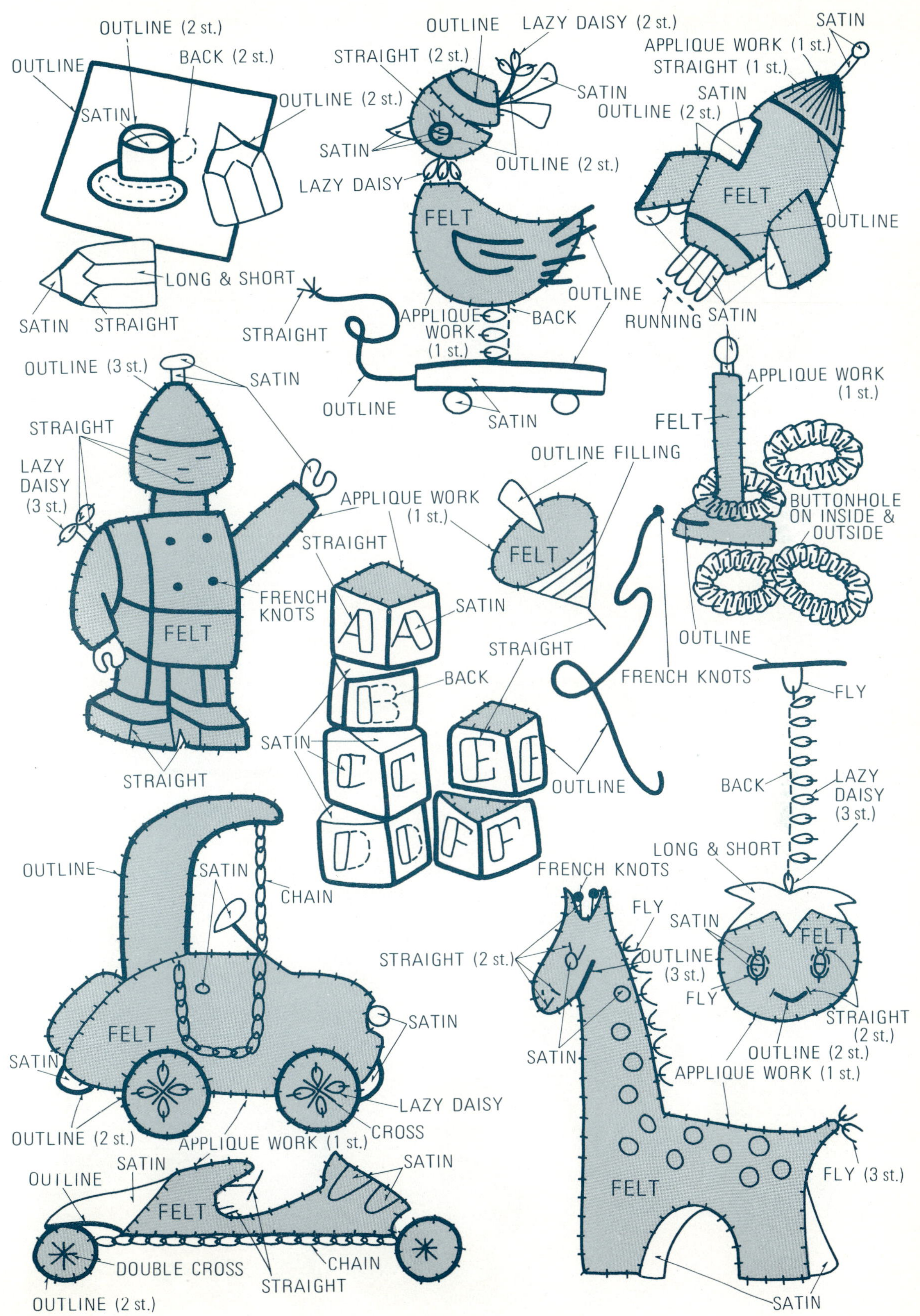

DELIGHTFUL VEHICLES

Designed by
MINAKO MORI

Designed by
MINAKO MORI

Shown on page 32. *(2 strands, unless otherwise specified)*

Shown on page 33. *(2 strands, unless otherwise specified)*

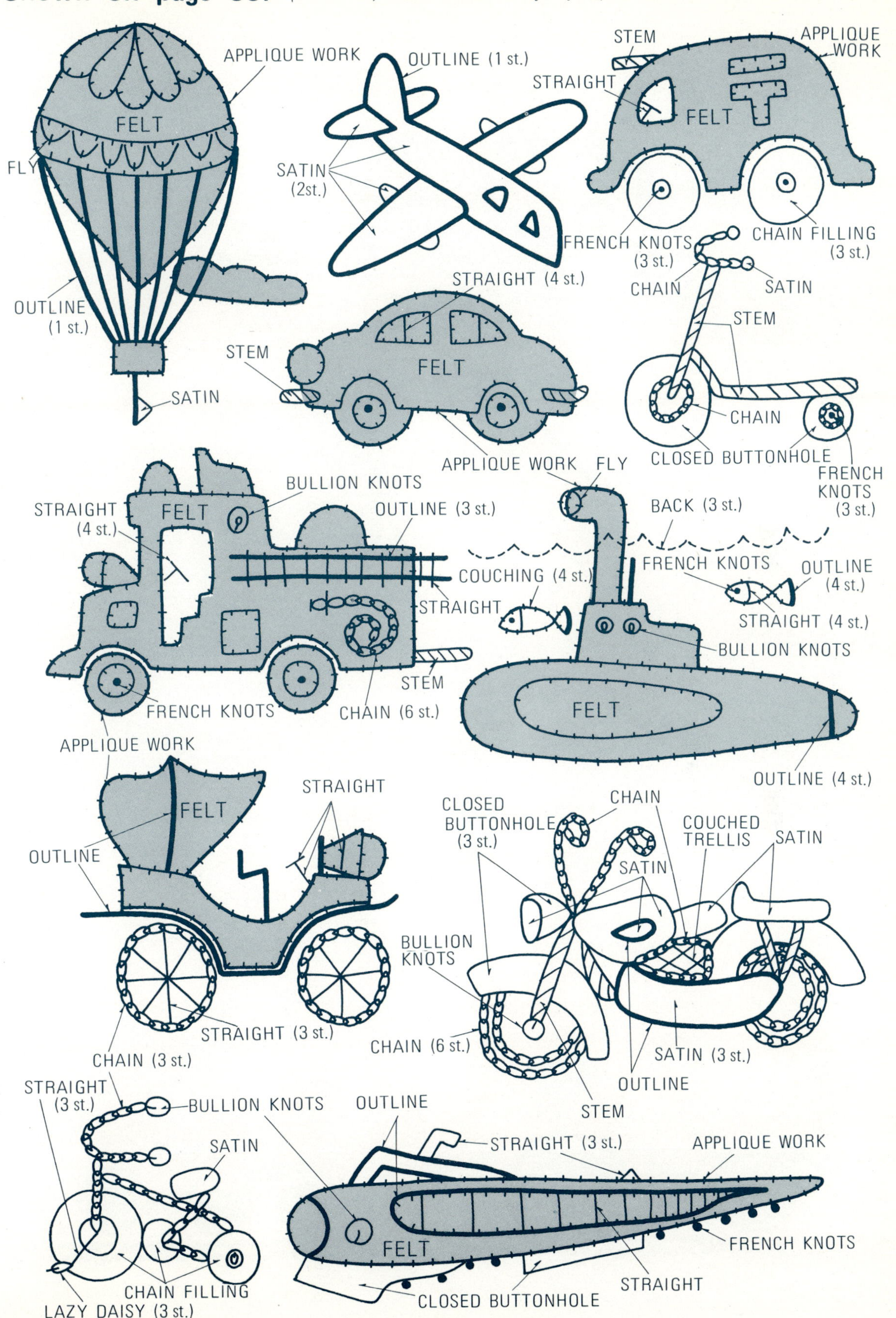

Designed by
SUMI AZUCHI

Designed by
SUMI AZUCHI

Shown on page 36. *(3 strands, unless otherwise specified)*

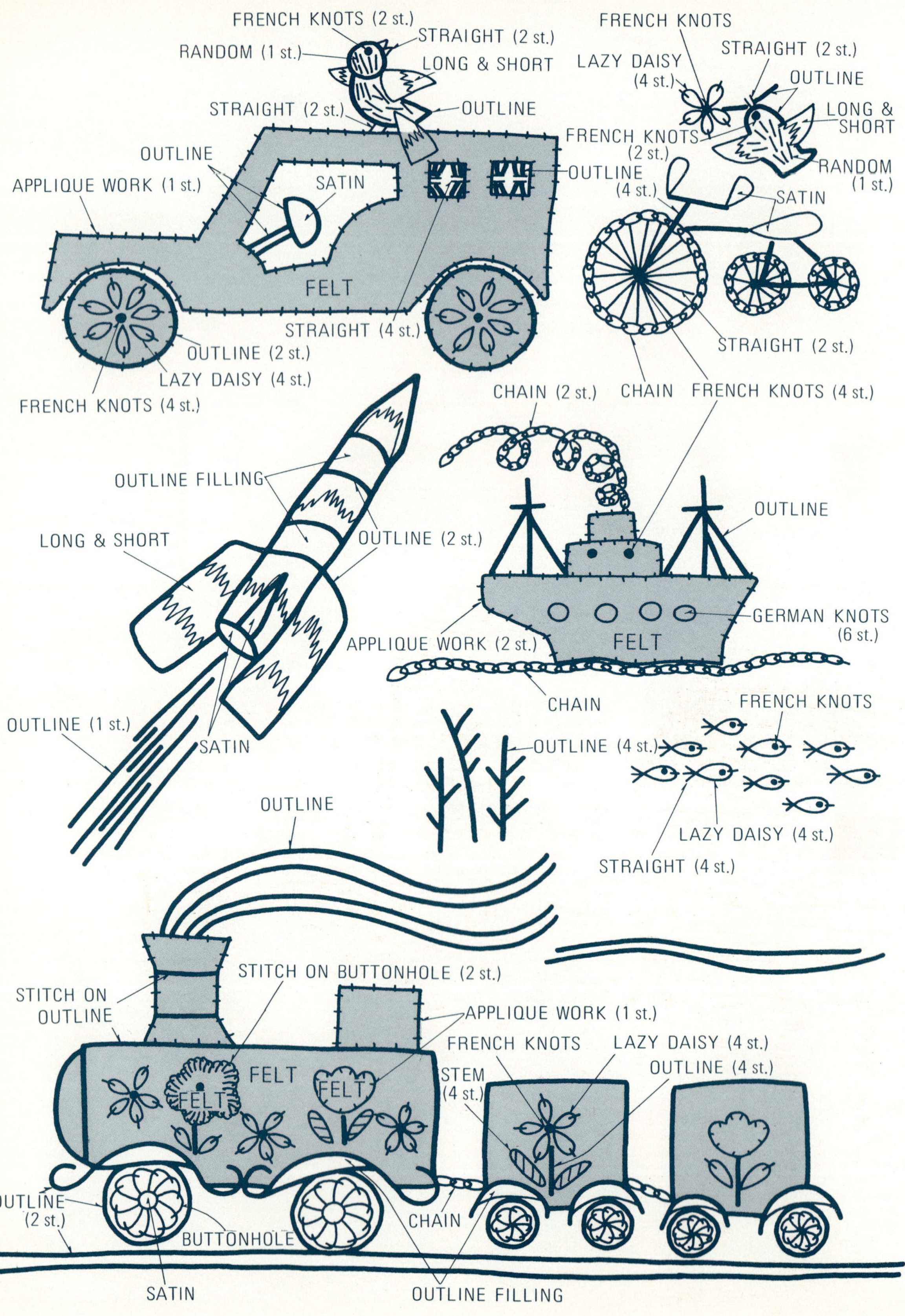

Shown on page 37. *(3 strands, unless otherwise specified)*

PUZZLES IN FIGURES

Designed by
FUMIKO NAKAYAMA

Designed by
FUMIKO NAKAYAMA

Shown on page 40. *(3 strands, unless otherwise specified)*

Shown on page 41. *(3 strands, unless otherwise specified)*

Designed by
MASANO ONOE

Designed by
MASANO ONOE

Shown on page 44. *(3 strands, unless otherwise specified)*

Shown on page 45. *(4 strands, unless otherwise specified)*

WHAT'S YOUR NAME?

Designed by
ISAO KIMURA

Designed by
ISAO KIMURA

Shown on page 48. *(3 strands, unless otherwise specified)*

Shown on page 49. *(3 strands, unless otherwise specified)*

Designed by
ETSUKO OSAKA

Designed by
ETSUKO OSAKA

Shown on page 52. *(3 strands, unless otherwise specified)*

Shown on page 53. *(3 strands, unless otherwise specified)*

THE ALPHABET

Designed by
FUMIE ITAGAKI

Designed by
FUMIE ITAGAKI

Shown on page 56. *(3 strands, unless otherwise specified)*

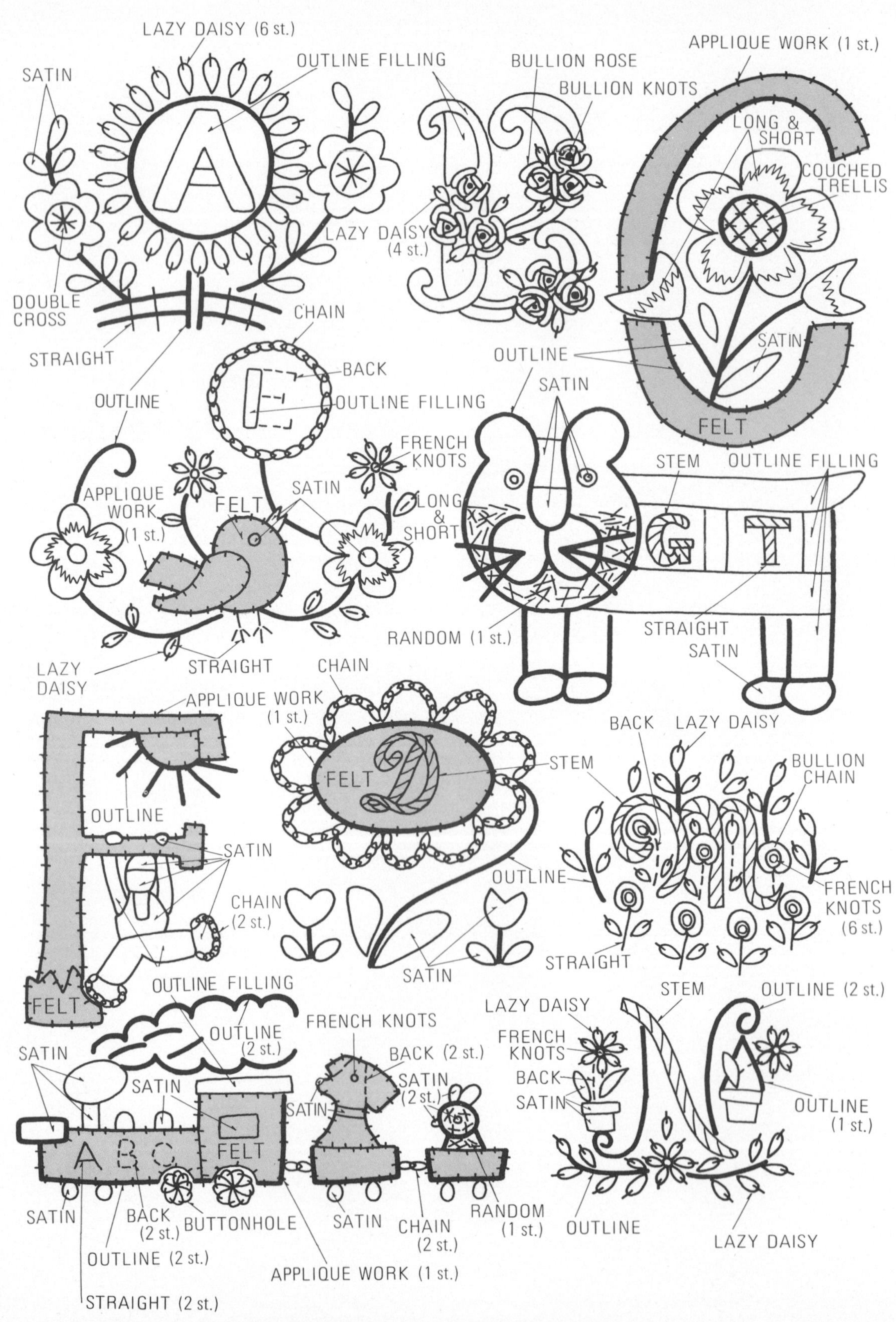

Shown on page 57. *(3 strands, unless otherwise specified)*

LOVELY BORDER PATTERNS

Designed by
NORIKO SUZUKI

Designed by
NORIKO SUZUKI

Shown on page 60. *(3 strands, unless otherwise specified)*

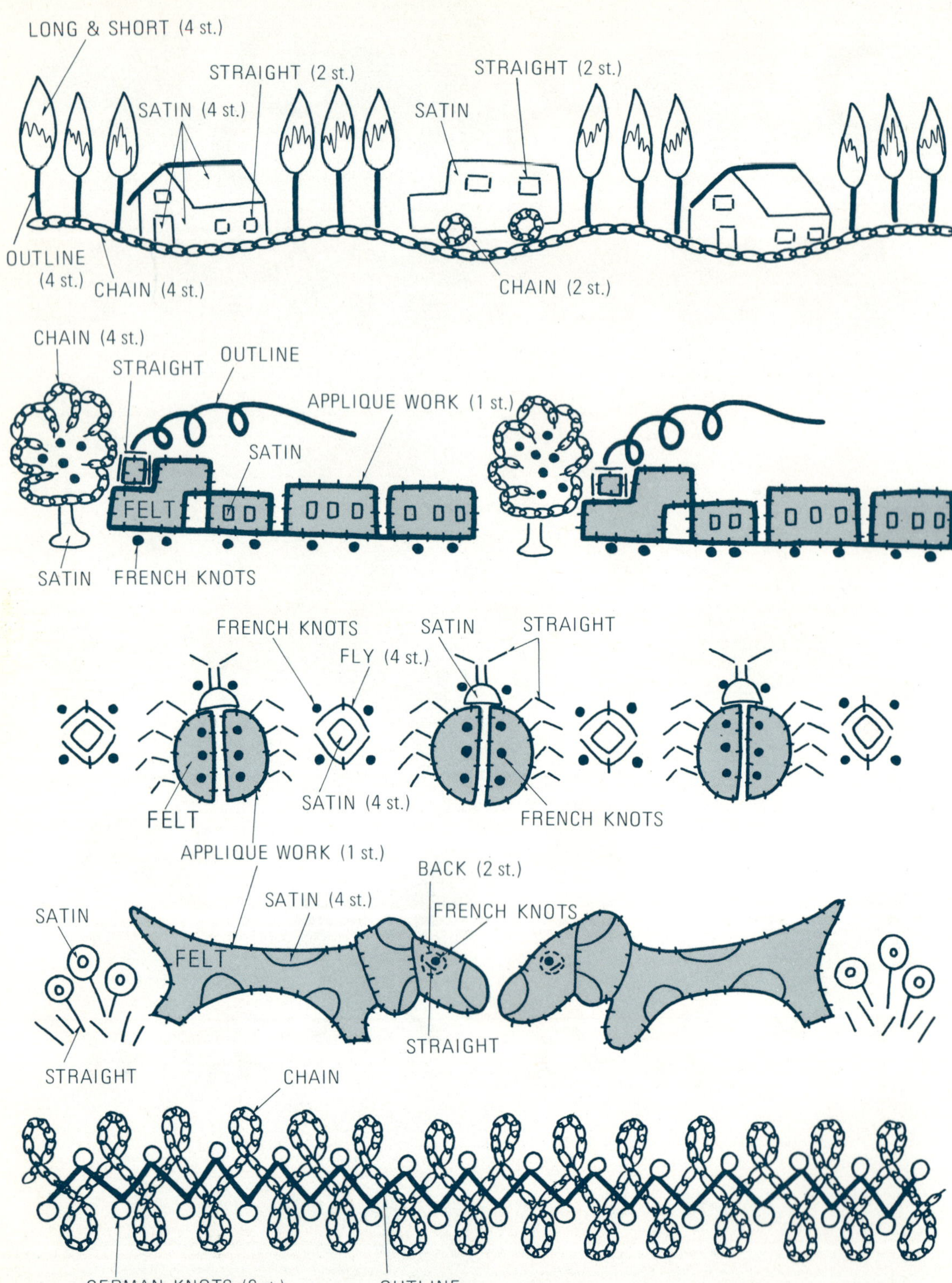

Shown on page 61. *(3 strands, unless otherwise specified)*

GIFTS FOR YOUR BABY

A sweet touch to your gift-giving for newborn babies. The contrasting designs worked on the baby's wear and the handkerchief of terry cloth; the pastel tone of nursing bottle cover; the baby's name embroidered on the album; these are all delightful things for young expectant mothers.

Designed by FUMIE ITAGAKI

Instructions; baby's dress is on page 77, baby's bib is on page 76, the cover of nursing bottle is on page 73, album is on page 74, napkin is on page 76.

FOR NAUGHTY CHILDREN

The hand made patch pockets attached on ready-made clothing. The appliques finished with embroidery are picked up from the fantasy world children love.

Designed by KEIKO KASHIWABARA
Instructions; jumper skirt is on page 78, overalls are on page 77, blouse is on page 80, purse is on page 79, hat is on page 80, vest is on page 78.

AT THE KINDERGARTEN

She is proud of her shoulder bag. The matching embroidery worked on yoke and bag makes her look more charming.
She loves the girl on her quilted hood and the rabbits on her lunch napkins. You may embroider name or initials for quick identification.

Designed by SETSUKO MITAMURA
Instructions; smock is on page 80, bag is on page 85, quilted hood is on page 84, the case or lunch box is on page 82, handkerchief is on page 83, cup case is on page 81.

Designed by MASANO ONOE

Instructions; wall hanging is on page 91, sack for exercise wear is on page 89, abacus case is on page 88, school bag is on page 87, pencil [illegible] is on page 86.

GRADE SCHOOL CHILDREN

FOR THE STYLISH TEEN-AGERS

Designed by YOSHIE TAKAMUNE

 Instructions; bag is on page 93, cushion is on page 94, vanity-case is on page 94.

✻ NURSING BOTTLE COVER Shown on page 65. ✻

***You'll Need:**

30 cm by 20 cm each of Cream linen, Cream flannelette. 40 cm of 1 cm White lace. D.M.C. Stranded Cotton: 1 skein of 725 (Saffron); small amount each of 703 (Brilliant Green), 741 (Tangerine Yellow), 956 (Peony Rose), 800, 821 (Sevres Blue), 310 (Black).

***Finished Size:** Refer to diagram.

***Making Instructions:**

Cut out-fabric as indicated, cut lining 0.3 cm smaller all around than the out fabric.

Work embroidery on out piece where marked.

Sew nursing bottle cover following to ①-③ pass string through, finish both ends in fringe.

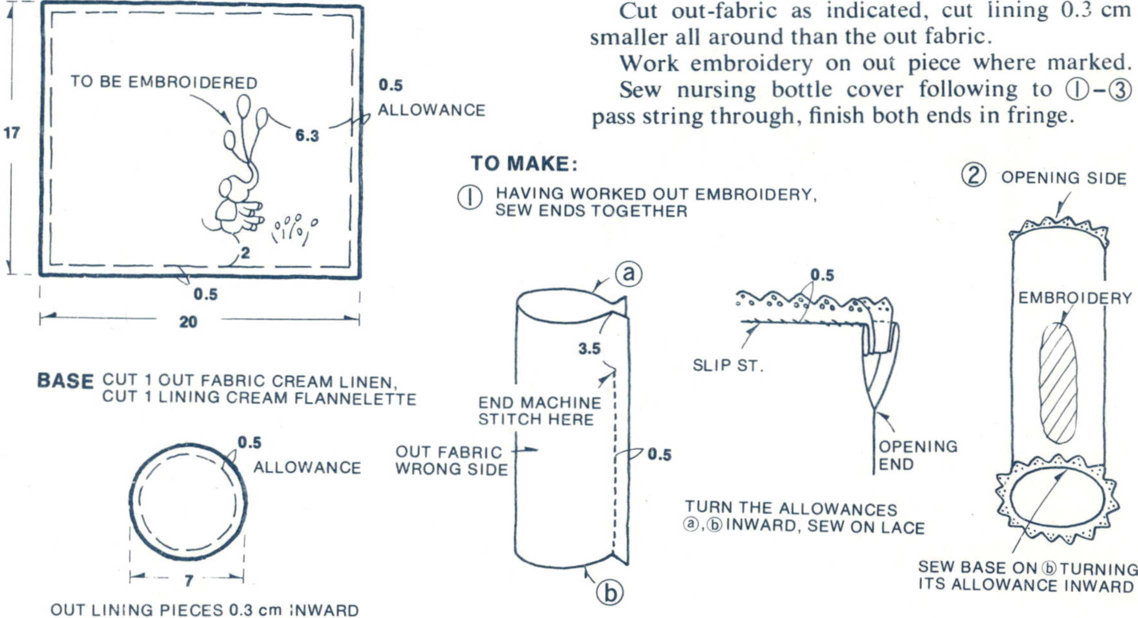

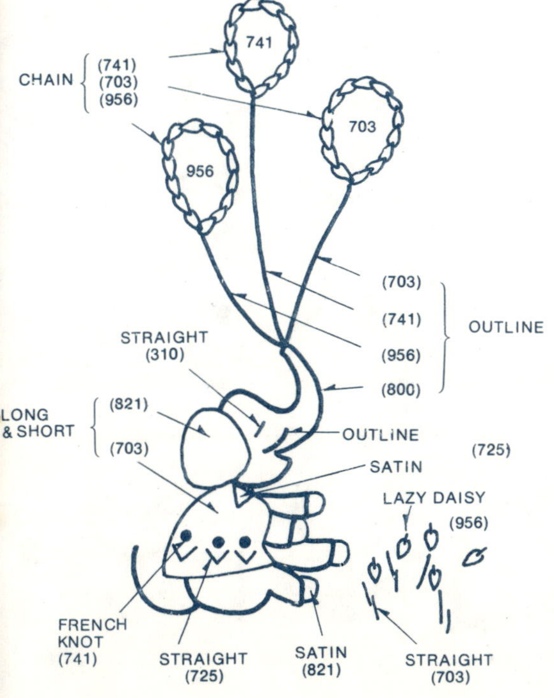

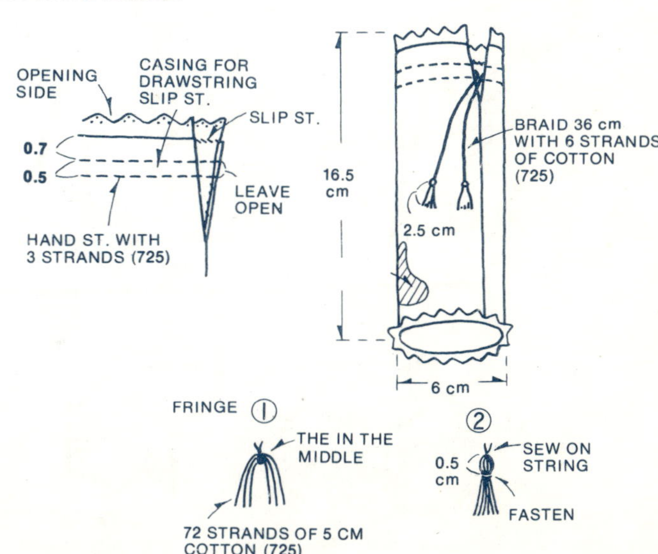

✲ ALBUM Shown on page 65. ✲

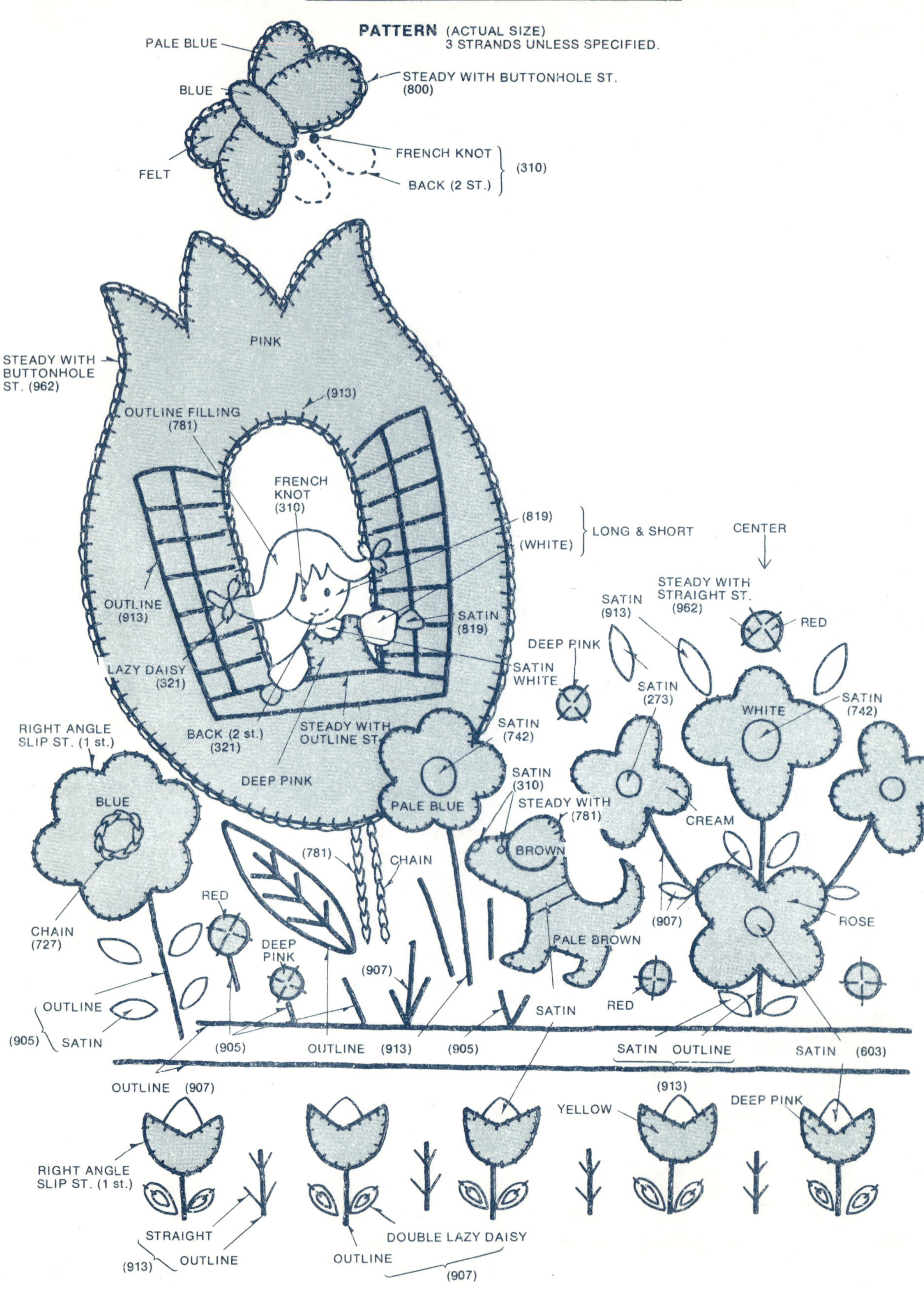

***You'll Need:**
90 cm by 45 cm Pink linen. Felt; 13 cm by 9 cm each of Pink, Yellow, 8 cm by 4 cm Pale Brown, 8 cm by 3 cm Deep Pink, 6 cm by 3 cm Cream, 8 cm square Blue, 6 cm by 4 cm Pale Blue, 4 cm square each of White, Rose, small amount each of Brown, Red. D.M.C. Stranded Cotton: ½ skein each of 798 (Sevres Blue), 905 & 907 (Parakeet Green), 913 (Emerald Green), 781 (Golden Yellow); small amount each of 602 & 603 (Cerise), 738 (Umber), 962 (Magenta Rose), 819 (Soft Pink), 727 (Saffron), 800 (Sevres Blue), 740 & 742 (Tangerine Yellow), 321 (Turkey Red), White, 310 (Black), Felt color.

***Finished Size:** 40 cm by 34.5 cm.

***Making Instructions:**

Refeering to the chart of layout, copy design on the fabric, work applique and embroidery. Having worked out every detail, take the piece to crafts-shop and ask for its finish.

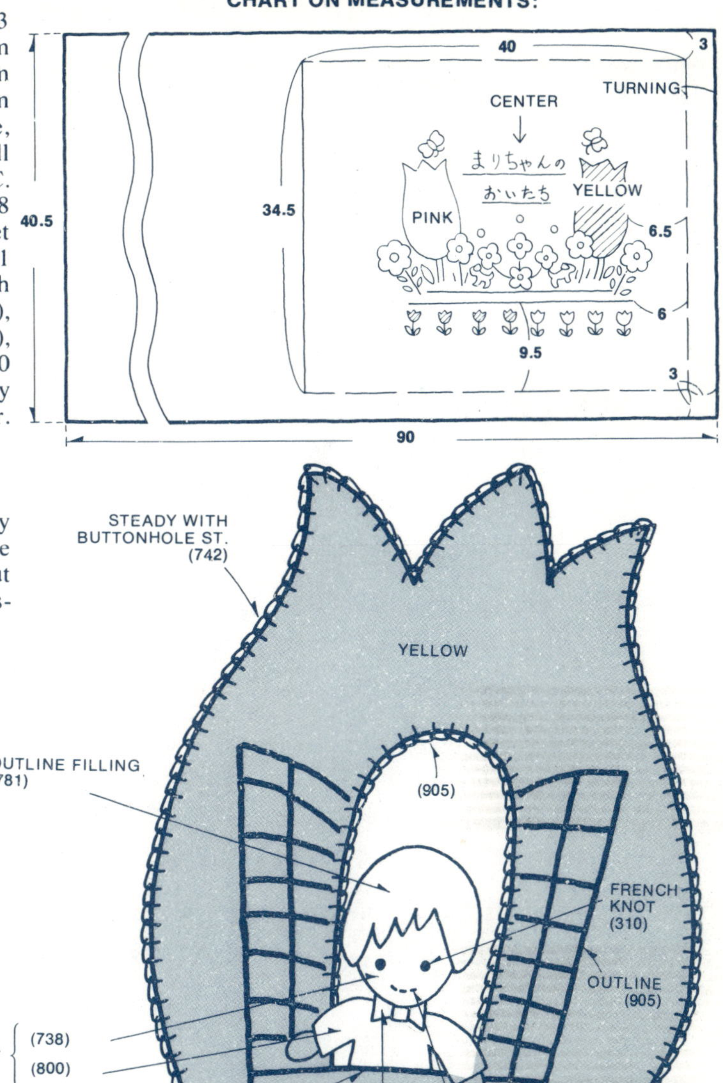

✲ BABY'S BIB Shown on page 64. ✲

***You'll Need:**

1 piece of ready-made bib of White jersey (22 cm long, 20 cm wide). D.M.C. Stranded Cotton: small amount each of 3688 (Raspberry Red), 740 (Tangerine Yellow), 945 (Aprikot Pink), 734 (Yellow Green), 827 (Forget-me-not Blue), 3326 (Soft Pink), 602–604 (Cerise), 957 (Peony Rose).

***Making Instructions:**

Copy design on the bib where decorate, work embroidery.

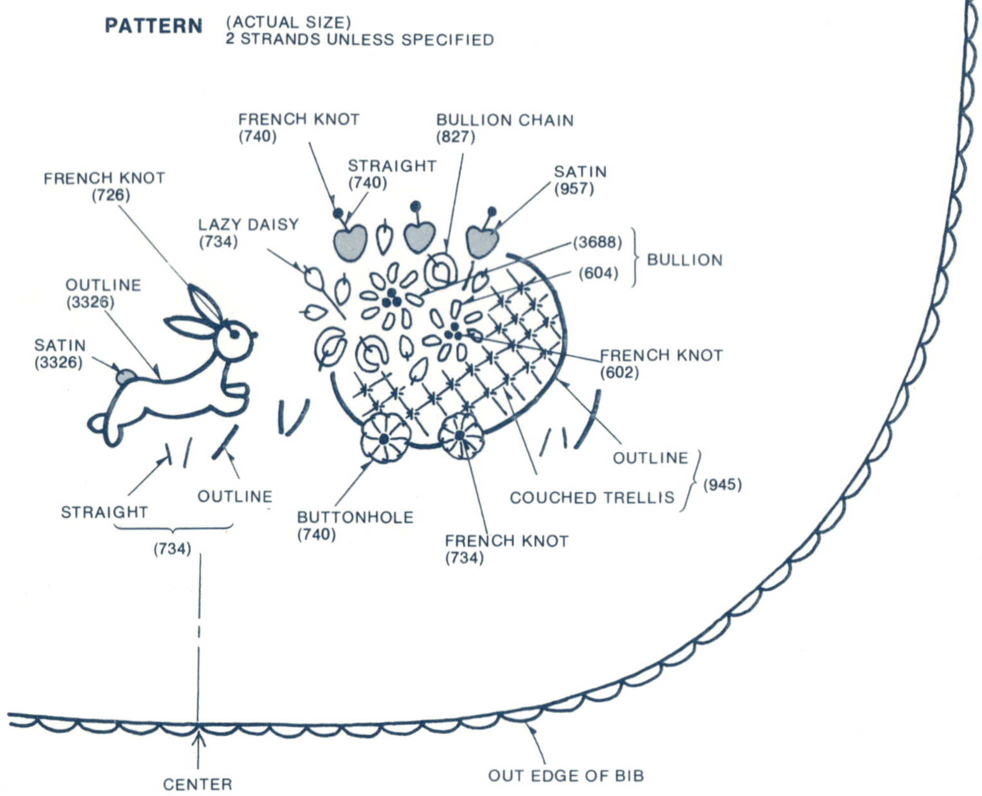

✲ NAPKIN Shown on page 65. ✲

***You'll Need:**

1 piece of 30 cm square handkerchief of White terry cloth. D.M.C. Stranded Cotton: small amount each of 3325 (Azure Blue), 827 (Forget-me-not Blue), 956 (Peony Rose), 912 (Emerald Green), 783 (Golden Yellow), 307 (Lemon Yellow), 310 (Black).

***Making Instructions:**

Copy design on handkerchief, work embroidery.

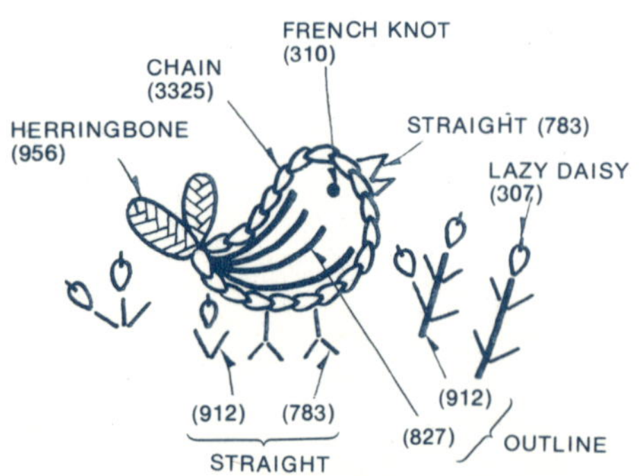

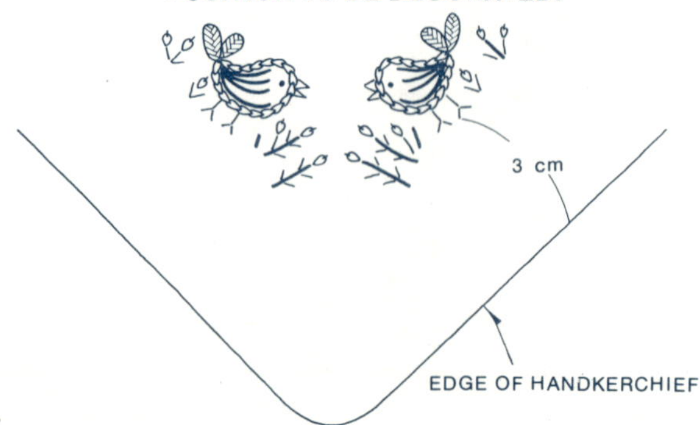

✱ BABY'S DRESS Shown on page 64. ✱

***You'll Need:**

1 piece of ready-made baby-dress of White jersey (Bust, 56 cm. Length, 62 cm. Sleeve length, 30 cm). D.M.C. Stranded Cotton: small amount each of 800 (Sevres Blue), 3348 (Scarab Green), 3689 Raspberry Red), 727 (Saffron).

***Making Instructions:**

Copy design on the dress where to decorate, work embroidery.

PATTERN (ACTUAL SIZE)

3 STRANDS UNLESS SPECIFIED

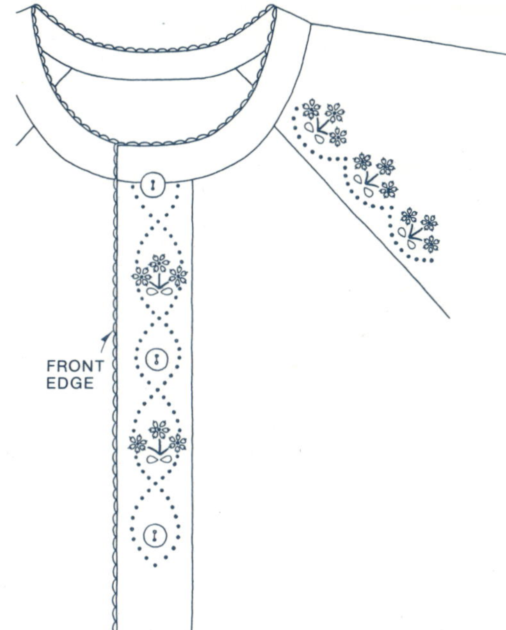

✱ OVERALLS Shown on page 66. ✱

***You'll Need:**

Denim pants of ready-made (Bust, 56 cm. Crotch length, 17 cm. Length below the crotch, 36 cm). Felt; 19 cm by 10 cm Dark Brown, 16 cm by 8 cm Red, 7 cm square Yellow, small amount each of Dark Blue, Green. D.M.C. Stranded Cotton: small amount each of 801 (Coffee Brown), 869 (Hazelnut Brown), 321 (Turkey Red), 823 (Indigo), Felt color.

***Making Instructions:**

Cut felt along design, work applique and embroidery on the pants knee position. Applique right and left symmetrically.

PATTERN
(ACTUAL SIZE)
3 STRANDS UNLESS SPECIFIED

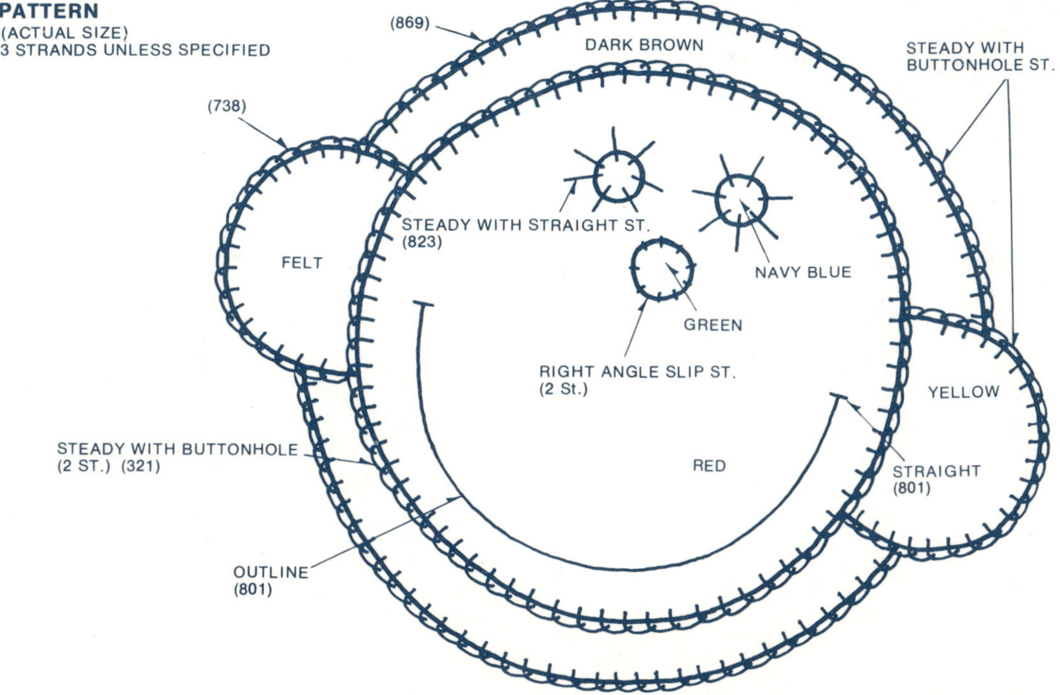

JUMPER SKIRT Shown on page 66.

***You'll Need:**
Ready-made jumper skirt of Red corduroy (Bust, 56 cm. Length, 45 cm). Felt; 4 cm by 3 cm each of White, Blue, small amount each of Pink, Green, Yellow, Pale Orange. D.M.C. Stranded Cotton: small amount each of White, 321 (Turkey Red), 801 (Coffee Brown), 796 (Royal Blue), Felt color. 2 of 1 cm diameter shell button.

***Making Instructions:**

Cut felt along design, work applique and embroidery on the breast of jumper skirt. Sew on wheels of button.

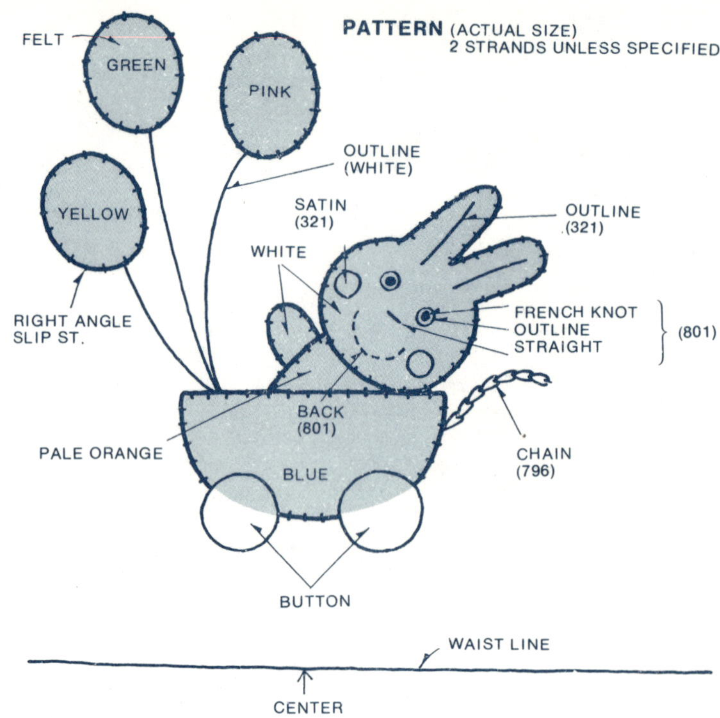

VEST Shown on page 66.

***You'll Need:**

Ready-made denim vest (Bust, 60 cm. Length, 28 cm. Shoulder tip to shoulder tip, 20 cm). Felt; 4 cm square Green, 3 cm square each of White, Dark Brown, small amount each of Yellow, Red, Pale Orange. D.M.C. Stranded Cotton: small amount each of White, 996 (Royal Blue), 742 (Tangerine Yellow), 321 (Turkey Red), 801 (Coffee Brown), Felt color.

***Making Instructions:**

Cut felt along design, work applique and embroidery on the pocket patched on the vest left front.

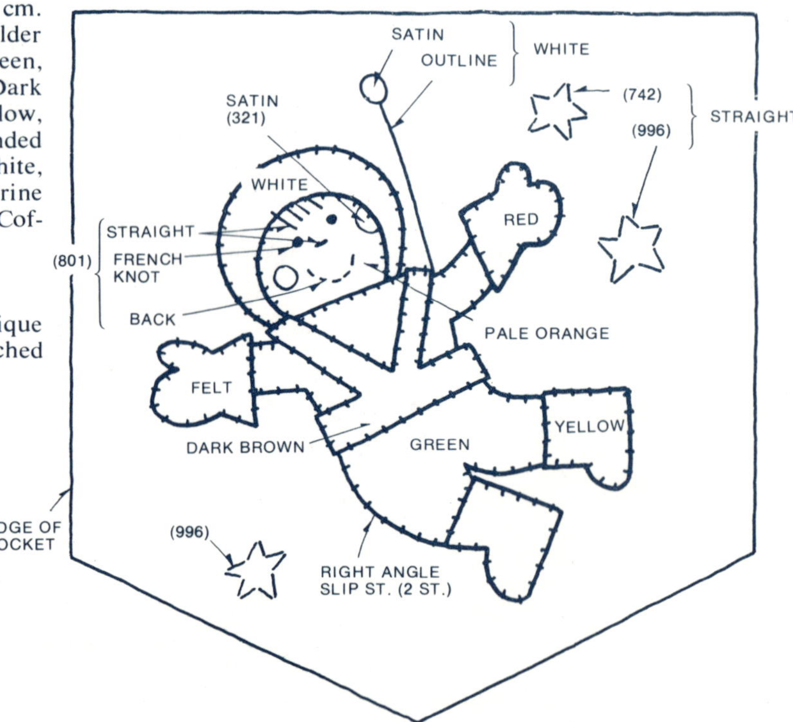

✻PURSE Shown on page 67. ✻

***You'll Need:**

40 cm by 25 cm each of Red heavy weight jersey, Red iron-on interfacing. 85 cm of 2 cm bias tape Dark Blue. Felt; 5 cm square White, small amount each of Green, Yellow, Pale Orange, Pink, Blue. D.M.C. Stranded Cotton: small amount each of 801 (Coffee Brown), 797 (Royal Blue), Felt color. 1 of 1.8 cm diameter Dark Blue button.

***Finished Size:** Refer to diagram.

***Making Instructions:**

Cut fabric following to the pattern, cut felt along design.

Make flap and sides following to ①–④, work applique and embroidery on the flap where to decorate. Make loop of button and shoulder belt, sew on referring to finished diagram.

PATTERN (ACTUAL SIZE)
2 STRANDS UNLESS SPECIFIED

YELLOW
STAIN (4 ST.)
(797)
STRAIGHT (4 ST.)
(801)
GREEN
PINK
RIGHT ANGLE
SLIP ST. (1 ST.)
OUTLINE
(801)
WHITE
OUTLINE
(797)
BLUE
PALE ORANGE

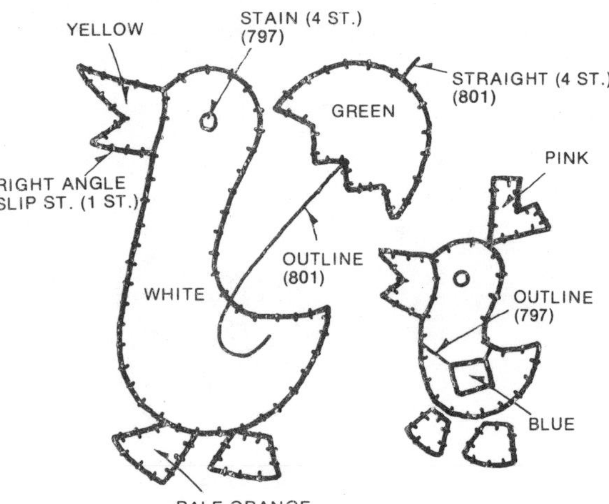

CUTTING:

CUT 1 FLAP FOLLOWING TO BACK,
CUT 1 FRONT (CUT PIECES OUT AFTER INTERFACING IS ATTACHED ON).

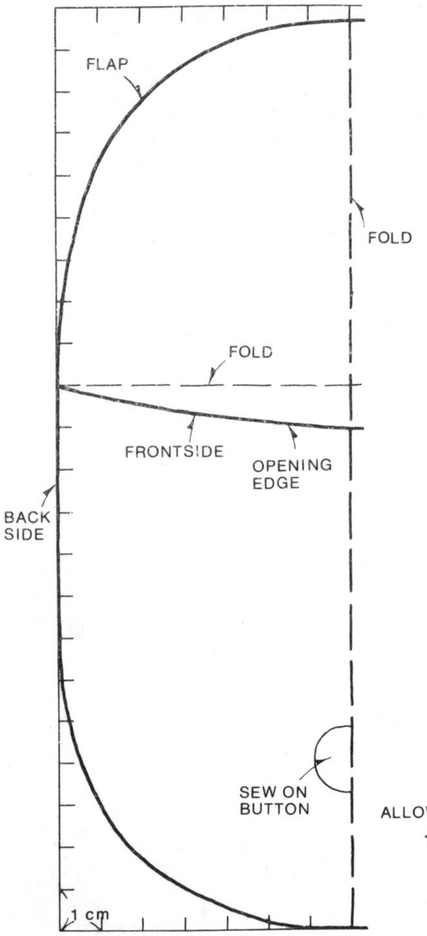

FLAP
FOLD
FOLD
FRONTSIDE
OPENING
EDGE
BACK
SIDE
SEW ON
BUTTON
1 cm

TO MAKE:

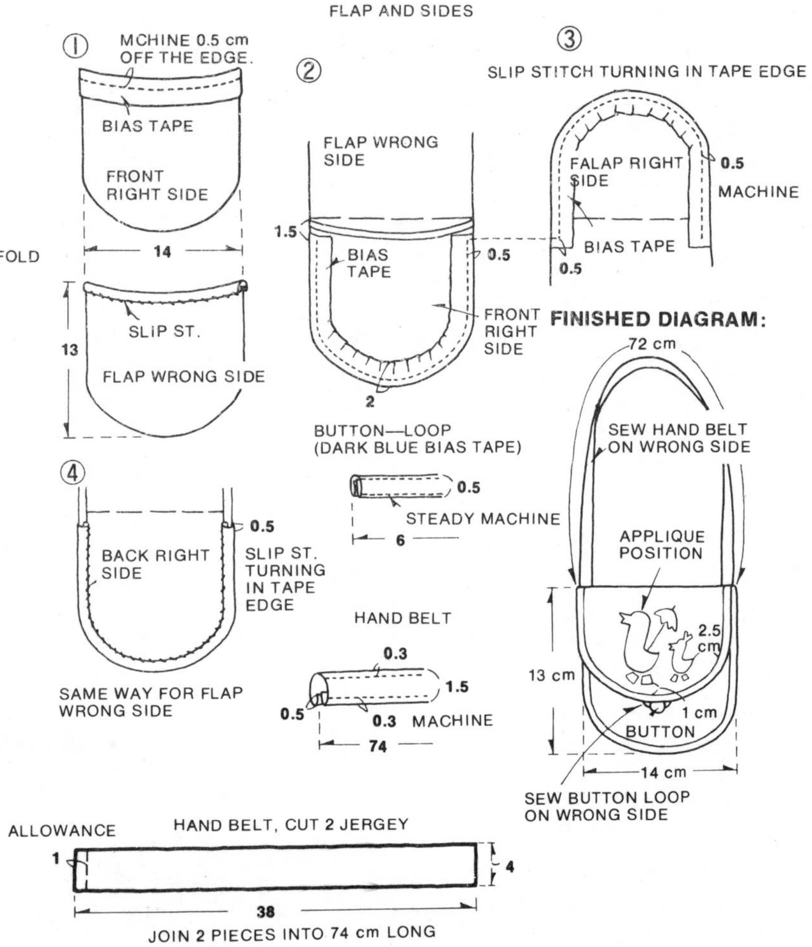

FLAP AND SIDES
①
MCHINE 0.5 cm
OFF THE EDGE.
BIAS TAPE
FRONT
RIGHT SIDE
14
13
SLIP ST.
FLAP WRONG SIDE
②
FLAP WRONG
SIDE
1.5
BIAS
TAPE
0.5
FRONT
RIGHT
SIDE
2
③
SLIP STITCH TURNING IN TAPE EDGE
FALAP RIGHT
SIDE
0.5
MACHINE
BIAS TAPE
0.5
④
BACK RIGHT
SIDE
0.5
SLIP ST.
TURNING
IN TAPE
EDGE
SAME WAY FOR FLAP
WRONG SIDE
BUTTON—LOOP
(DARK BLUE BIAS TAPE)
0.5
STEADY MACHINE
6
HAND BELT
0.3
1.5
0.5
0.3 MACHINE
74
ALLOWANCE
HAND BELT, CUT 2 JERGEY
1
4
38
JOIN 2 PIECES INTO 74 cm LONG
FINISHED DIAGRAM:
72 cm
SEW HAND BELT
ON WRONG SIDE
APPLIQUE
POSITION
2.5
cm
13 cm
1 cm
BUTTON
14 cm
SEW BUTTON LOOP
ON WRONG SIDE

✱BLOUSE Shown on page 67. ✱

***You'll Need:**

Ready-made blouse of White jersey (Bust, 60 cm. Length, 43 cm. Shoulder tip to shoulder tip, 25 cm. Sleeve length, 30 cm). D.M.C. Stranded Cotton: small amount each of 321 (Turkey Red), 973 (Canary Yellow), 699 (Brilliant Green), 470 (Moss Green).

***Making Instructions:**

Work embroidery on the blouse in front between pin tucks as shown.

PATTERN (ACTUAL SIZE) 3 STRANDS

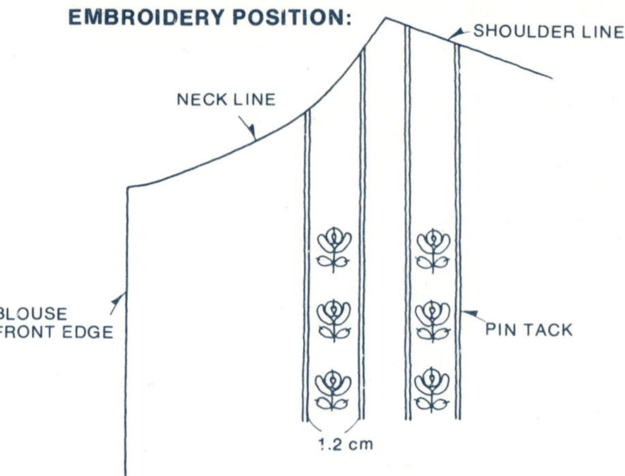

BULLION CHAIN (973)
BULLION (321)
LAZY DAISY (699)
STRAIGHT (470)

✱HAT Shown on page 67. ✱

***You'll Need:**

Ready-made denim hat (Round the head fullest part, 52 cm). Felt; small amount each of Red, Green, Brown, Blue. D.M.C. Stranded Cotton: small amount each of Felt colors. 2 of 0.7 cm diameter Gold Yellow button.

***Making Instructions:**

Cut felt along design, applique on the pocket patched on the crown of hat with right angle slip-stich, sew on wheels of button.

PATTERN (ACTUAL SIZE) 1 STRAND

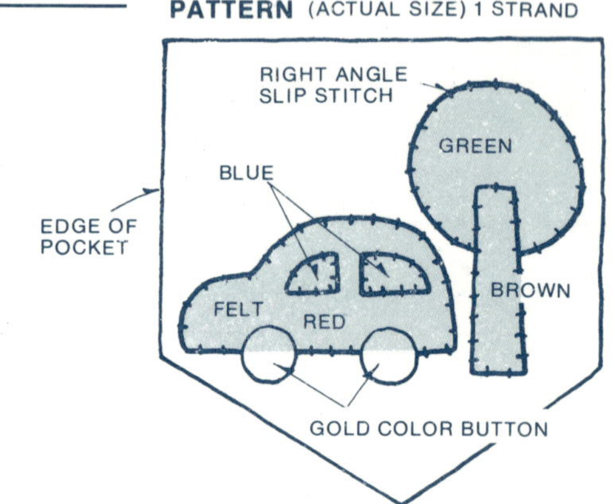

✱SMOCK Shown on page 68. ✱

***You'll Need:**

90 cm by 90 cm Dark Blue and White striped broad cloth. 65 cm by 30 cm Dark Blue broad cloth. D.M.C. Stranded Cotton: ½ skein of White; small amount each of 517 (Sky Blue), 666 (Poppy), 642 (Smoke Gray), 754 (Geranium Red), 702 (Brilliant Green). 4 of 1.5 cm diameter White button. 30 cm of elastic.

***Finished Size:**

Bust, 87 cm (includes gathering amount). Length, 45 cm. Shoulder tip to shoulder tip, 26 cm. Sleeve length, 33 cm.

***Making Instructions:**

Cut fabric referring to the chart of cutting, copy design referring to 1 for its position

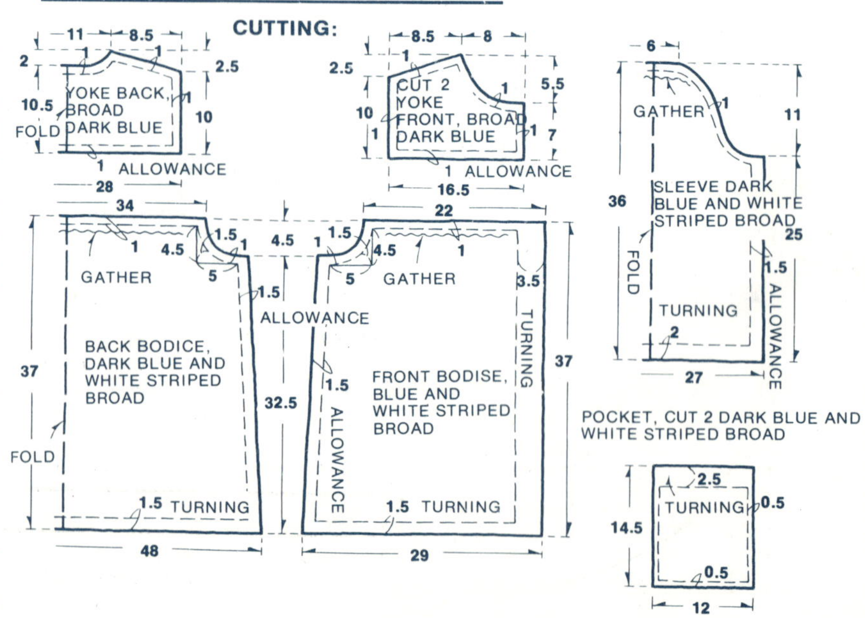

on the yoke, work embroidery.

Make into smock following to ①–④, slash buttonholes and stich along.

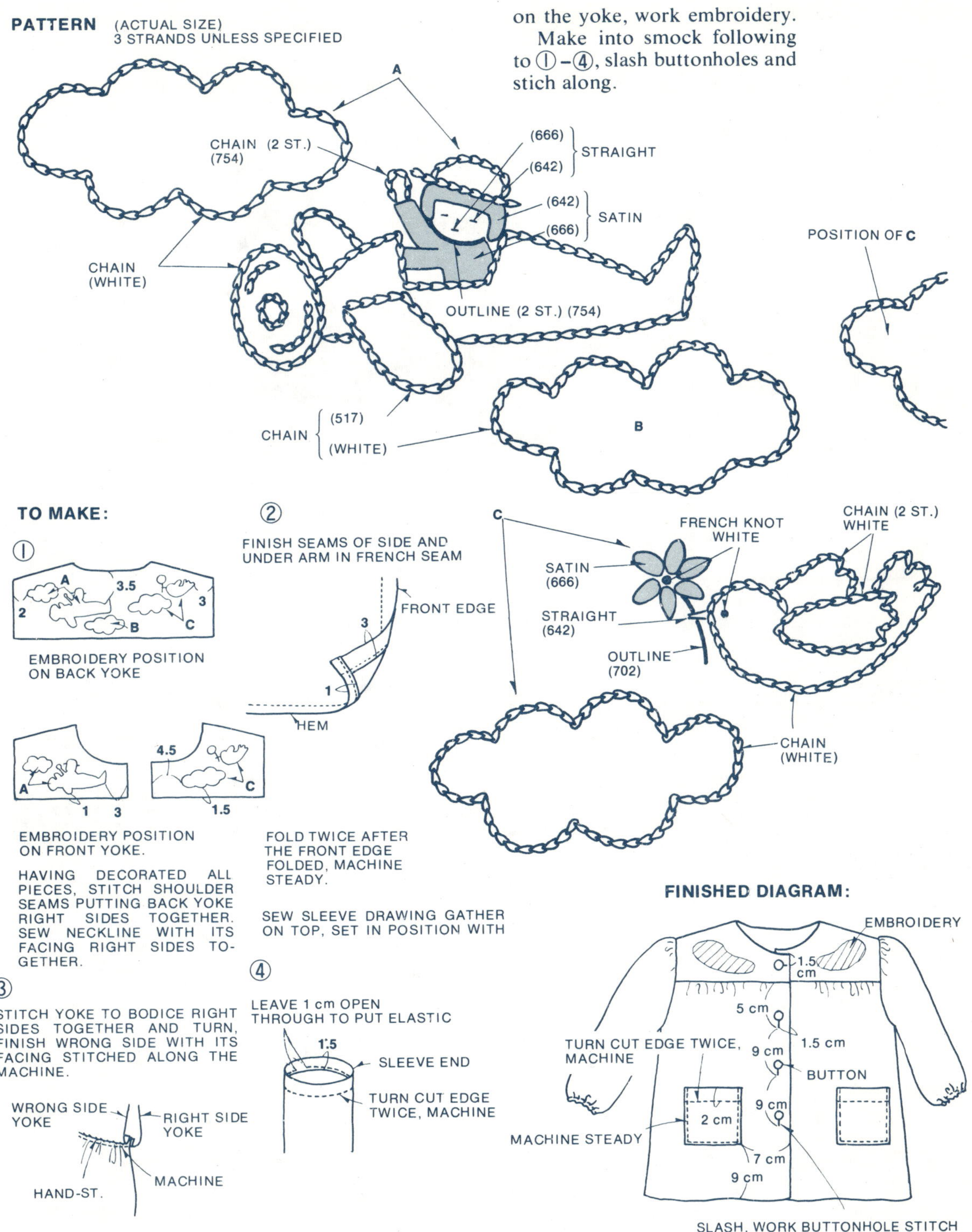

✻ CUP CASE Shown on page 69. ✻

***You'll Need:**

35 cm by 20 cm Yellow broad cloth. D.M.C. Stranded Cotton: small amount each of 957 (Peony Rose), 961 (Magenta Rose), 322 (Indigo), White. 80 cm of 0.4 cm diameter unbleached cord.

***Finished Size:** Refer to diagram.

***Making Instructions:**

Embroider the fabric where indicated, make into case refferring to diagrams, cut cord in half, pass them through as shown.

CHART ON MEASUREMENTS **PATTERN** (ACTUAL SIZE) 3 STRANDS

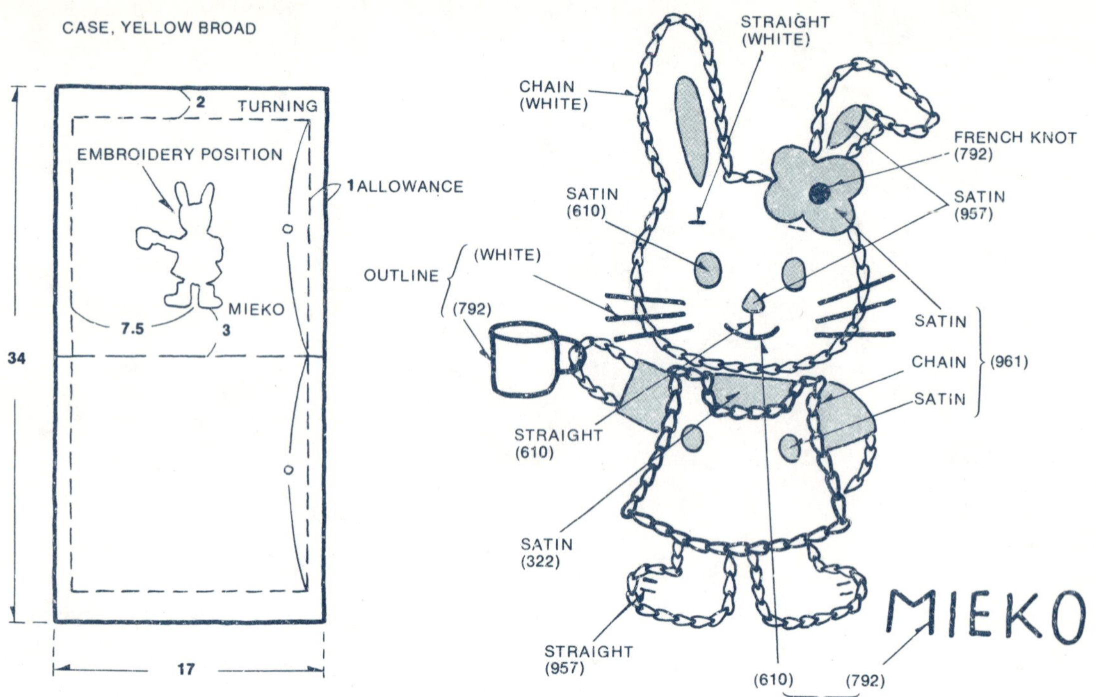

TO MAKE:

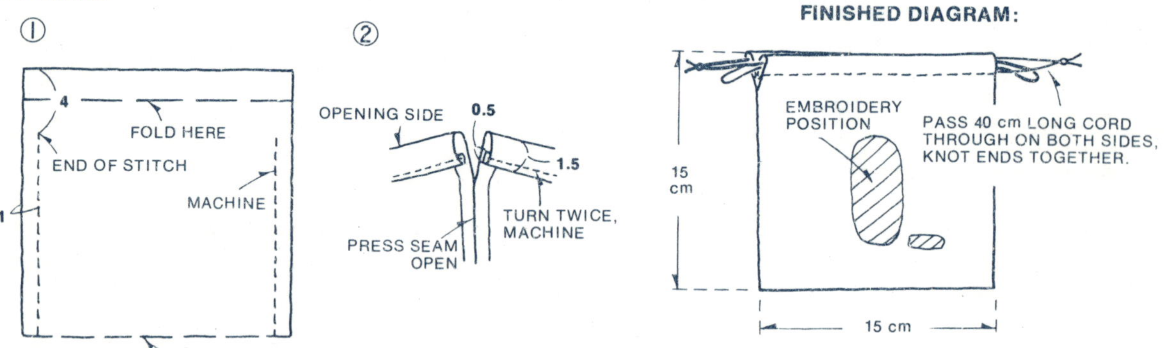

✻ LUNCH BOX CASE Shown on page 69. ✻

***You'll Need:**

30 cm square each of broad cloth Yellow, Pink. D.M.C. Stranded Cotton: small amount each of 957 (Peony Rose), 961 (Magenta Rose), 792 (Cornflower Blue), 322 (Indigo), 610 (Drab), White. 5 cm of 2.5 cm Instant Fastener (tape).

***Finished Size:** Refer to diagram.

***Making Instructions:**

Work embroidery on the out fabric where indicated, sew following to ①–③, sew on instant Fastener (tape).

CHART ON MEASUREMENTS:

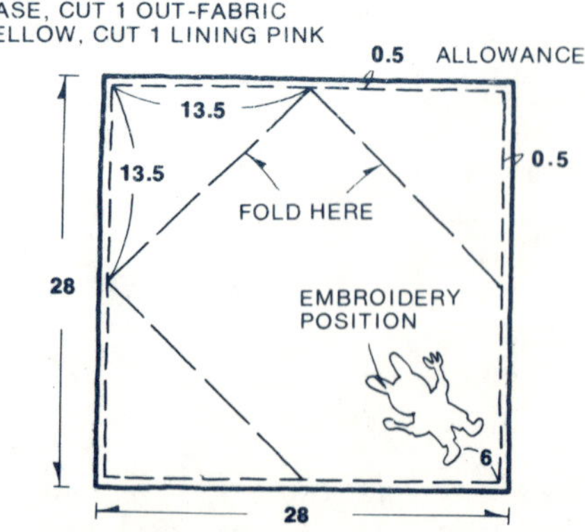

PATTERN (ACTUAL SIZE) 3 STRANDS

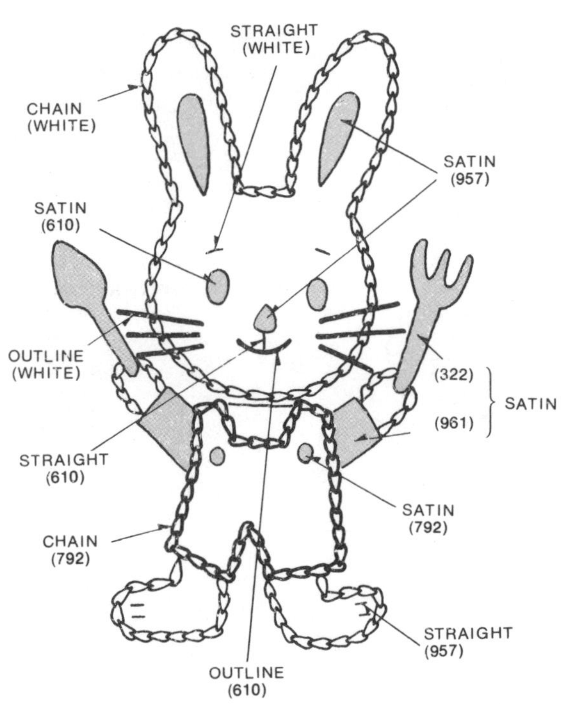

TO MAKE:

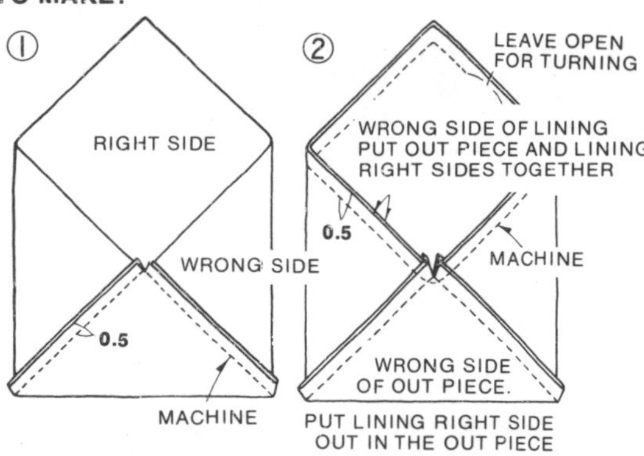

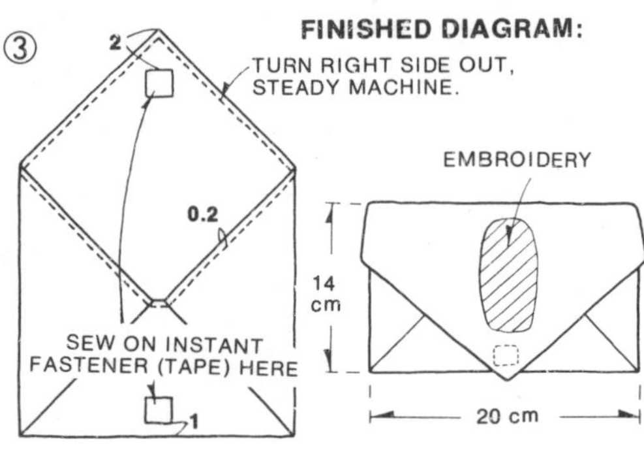

✻ HANDKERCHIEF Shown on page 68. ✻

***You'll Need:**

29 cm by 43 cm terry cloth handkerchief of Lemon Yellow. 5 cm square each of terry cloth Orange, Cherry Pink. D.M.C. Stranded Cotton: small amount each of 912 (Emerald Green), 433 (Umber), 792 (Cornflower Blue), Terry cloth color in applique.

***Finished Size:** Refer to diagram.

***Making Instructions:**

Cut applique pieces out from terry cloth 1 each in Orange, Cherry Pink with 0.5 cm allowance, applique on the handkerchief where indicated, embroider as shown.

CHART ON MEASUREMENTS:

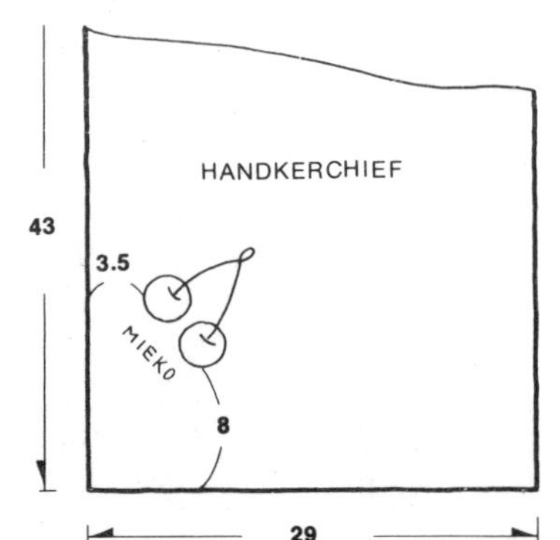

PATTERN

·CUT TERRY CLOTH PUTTING 0.5 cm ALLOWANCE

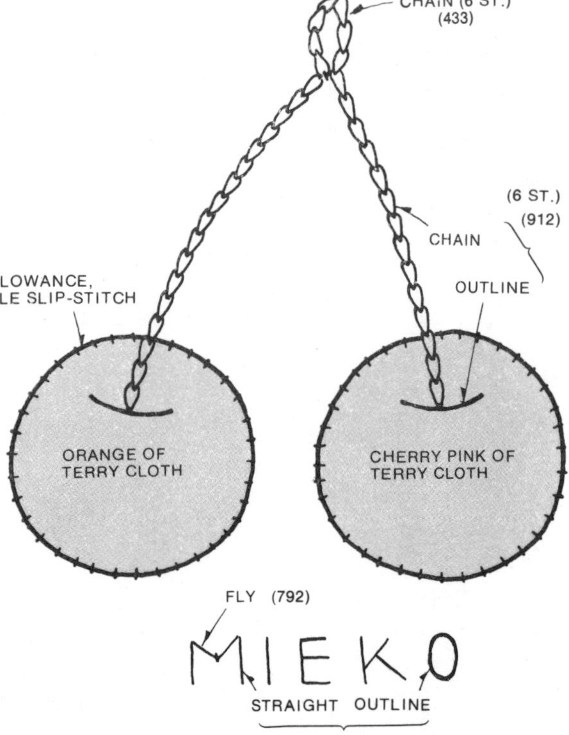

✲ QUILTED HOOD Shown on page 69.✲

PATTERN (ACTUAL SIZE)
3 STRANDS UNLESS SPECIFIED

***You'll Need:**

100 cm by 50 cm each of Dark Blue denim, Dark Blue broad cloth. Felt; 10 cm square Red, 7 cm by 3 cm Yellow, 7 cm by 2 cm Brown. D.M.C. Stranded Cotton: ½ skein of 666 (Poppy); small amount each of 726 (Saffron), 700 (Brilliant Green), 680 (Old Gold), 754 (Geranium Red), 956 (Peony Rose), 517 (Sky Blue), 783 (Golden Yellow), White, Felt color. 200 grams wadding.

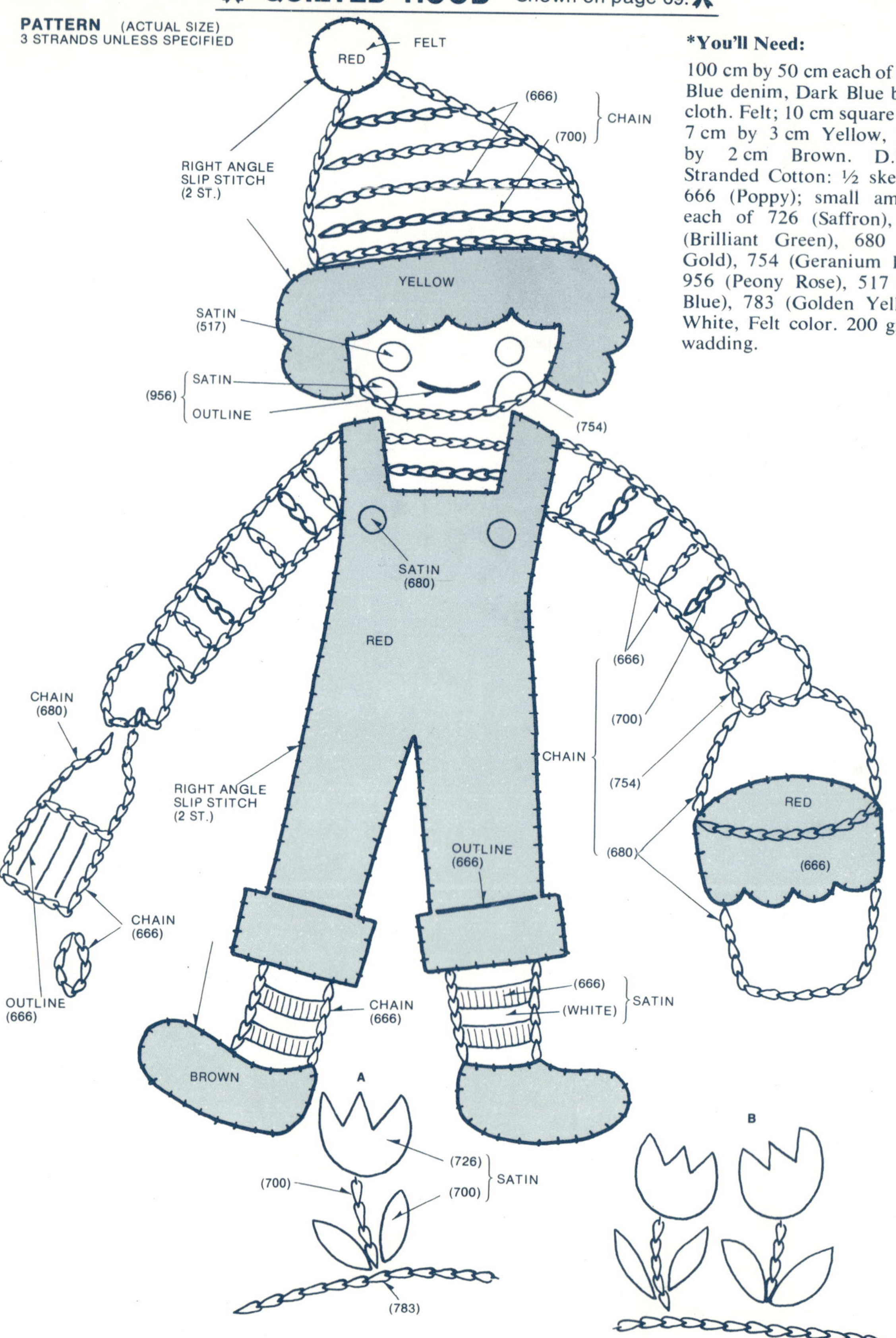

***Finished Size:** Refer to diagram.

***Making Instructions:**

Cut out-fabric referring to the chart of cutting, cut felt for applique following to design.

Having worked out embroidery and applique on the out fabric, sew following to ①–③, complete referring to finished diagram.

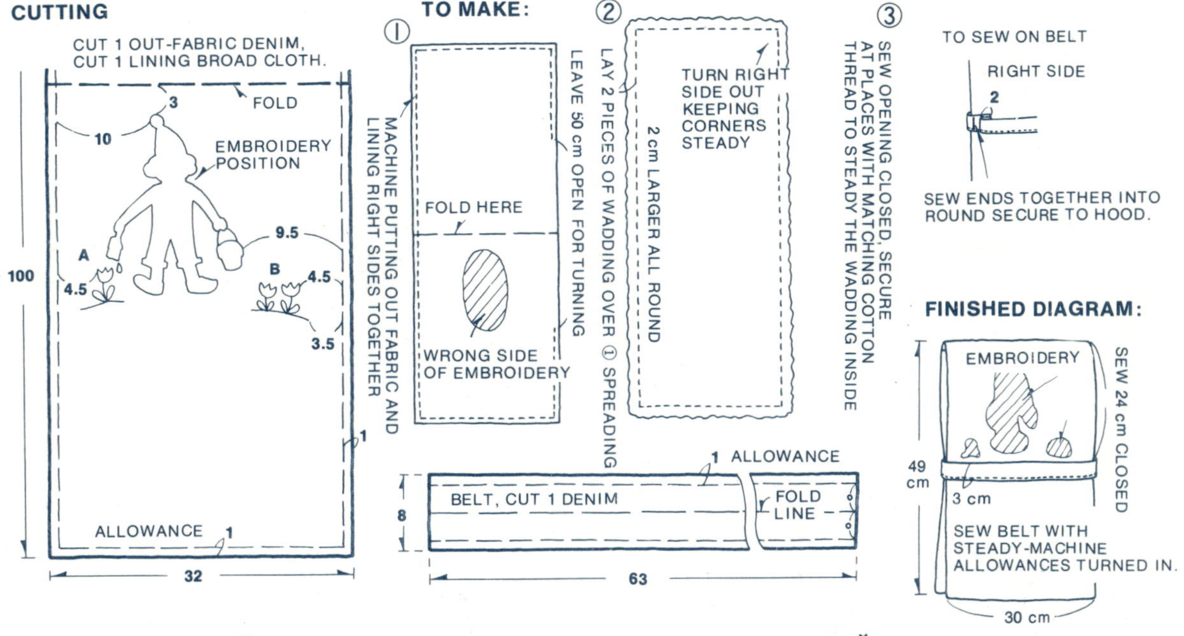

✲ SHOULDER BAG Shown on page 68. ✲

***You'll Need:**

80 cm by 30 cm Dark Blue denim. 30 cm by 25 cm broad print. Felt; 6 cm by 3 cm Red, 5 cm by 3 cm White, Brown scrap. D.M.C. Stranded Cotton: small amount each of 905 (Parakeet Green), 831 (Copper Green), 946 (Fire Red), 741 (Tangerine Yellow), 666 (Poppy), White, 444 (Buttercup Yellow), 611 (Drab), Felt color.

***Finished Size:** Refer to diagram.

***Making Instructions:**

Cut out pieces referring to the chart of cutting, sew into bag after the flap outside is decorated.

Make following to ①–③, finish with hand belt stitched on.

CUTTING: OUT FABRIC DENIM

3 3 1 2
FLAP
EMBROIDERY POSITION
2.5
1
FOLD LINE
0.3 SEW ON HAND BELT HERE 15
49
BACK FOLD LINE 1
FRONT 15
3 TURNING
22

LINING

3 1
FLAP, DENIM
19
1
1
ALLOWANCE
22
1
BACK (BROAD CLOTH) 13
28
FOLD LINE
FRONT 13
1 ALLOWANCE
22

HAND BELT, DENIM
6.5
1
1 TURNING
80

TO MAKE:

① MACHINE SIDES OF OUT FABRIC AND LINING RESPECTIVELY PUTTING FRONT AND BACK RIGHT SIDES TOGETHER.

FINSIHED DIAGRAM:

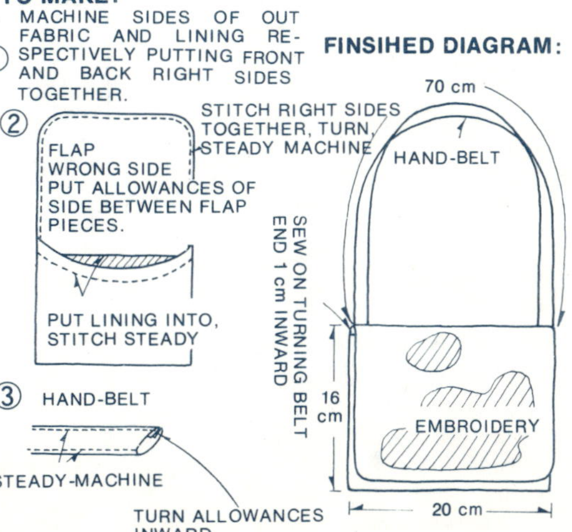

PATTERN (ACTUAL SIZE), 3 STRANDS UNLESS SPECIFIED.

CHAIN (741) (946)
FELT WHITE
RIGHT ANGLE SLIP-STITCH (2 ST.)
STRAIGHT (741)
FRENCH KNOT (611)
SATIN (741)
CHAIN (946) (666)
CHAIN (946)
FRENCH KNOT (666) (946)
RED
SATIN (741) (946)
BROWN
SATIN CHAIN (905)
(666) (444)
FRENCH KNOTS FILLING
FRENCH KNOT (741)
(WHITE) (905) (831)
CHAIN

✲PENCIL CASE Shown on page 74. ✲

***You'll Need:**

35 cm square Red cotton fabric. 30 cm by 20 cm striped cotton heavy weight. Felt; 8 cm by 6 cm Light Purple, 4 cm square each of Yellow, Beige, White. 3 cm square Black. D.M.C. Stranded Cotton: small amount each of 310 (Black), Felt color.

***Finished Size:** Refer to diagram.

***Making Instructions:**

Cut fabric pieces referring to the chart of cutting, cut felt for applique following design.

Work applique on out fabric, make following to ①–③.

CUTTING:

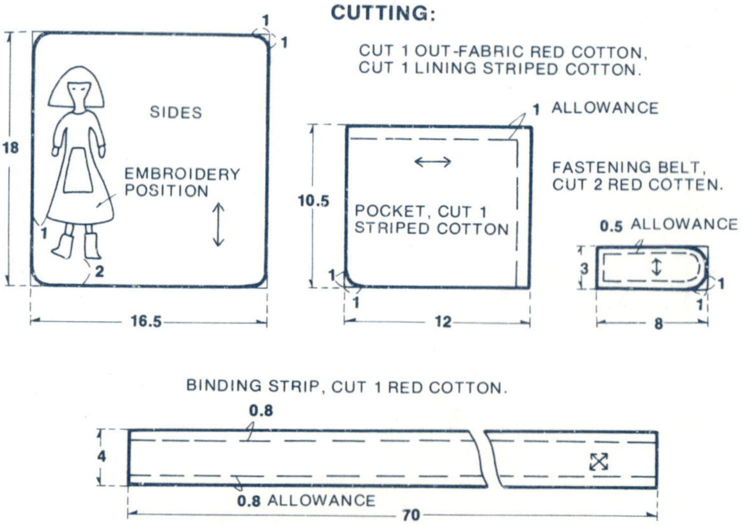

CUT 1 OUT-FABRIC RED COTTON,
CUT 1 LINING STRIPED COTTON.

SIDES
EMBROIDERY POSITION
18
16.5
1
2

POCKET, CUT 1 STRIPED COTTON
1 ALLOWANCE
10.5
12

FASTENING BELT, CUT 2 RED COTTEN.
0.5 ALLOWANCE
3
8

BINDING STRIP, CUT 1 RED COTTON.

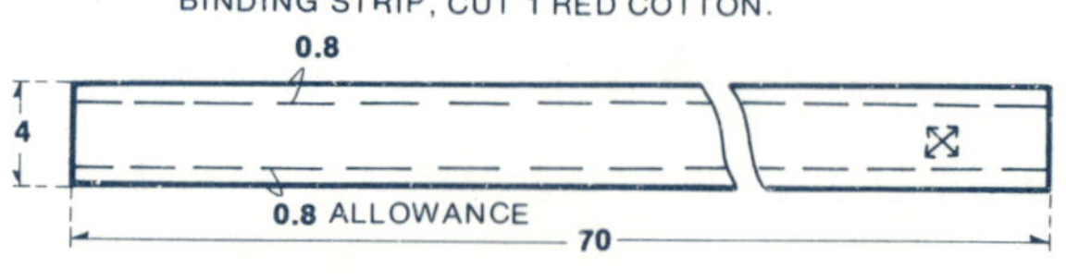

PATTERN
(ACTUAL SIZE)

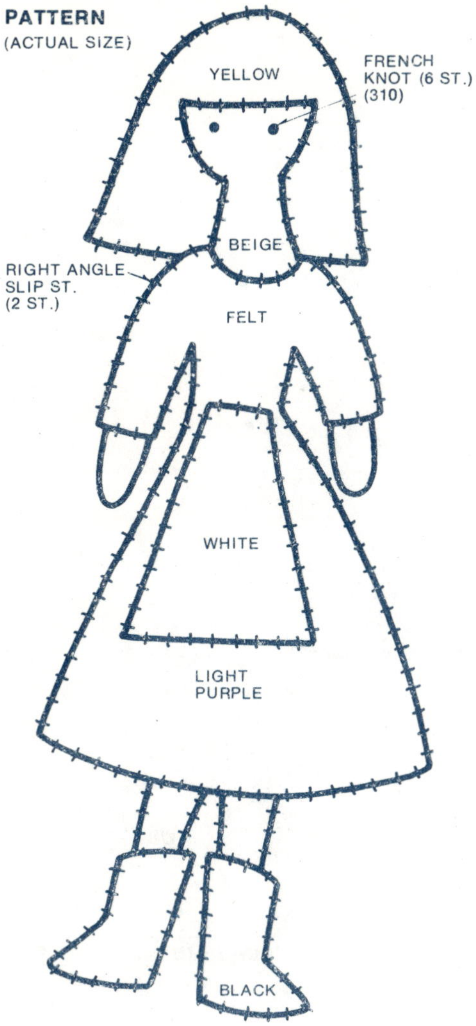

YELLOW
FRENCH KNOT (6 ST.) (310)
BEIGE
RIGHT ANGLE SLIP ST. (2 ST.)
FELT
WHITE
LIGHT PURPLE
BLACK

TO MAKE:

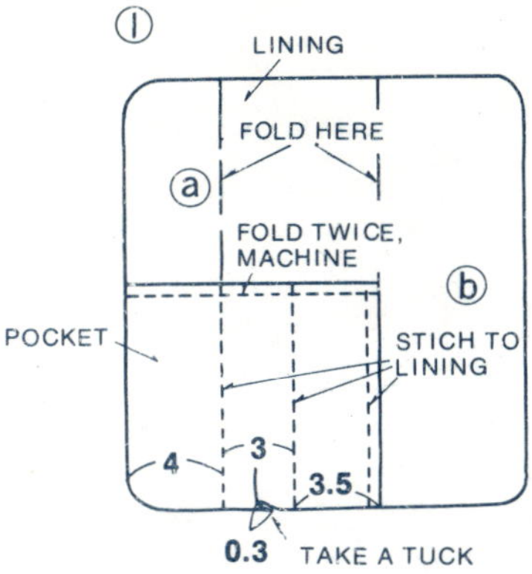

①
LINING
FOLD HERE
ⓐ
FOLD TWICE, MACHINE
ⓑ
POCKET
STICH TO LINING
4
3
3.5
0.3
TAKE A TUCK

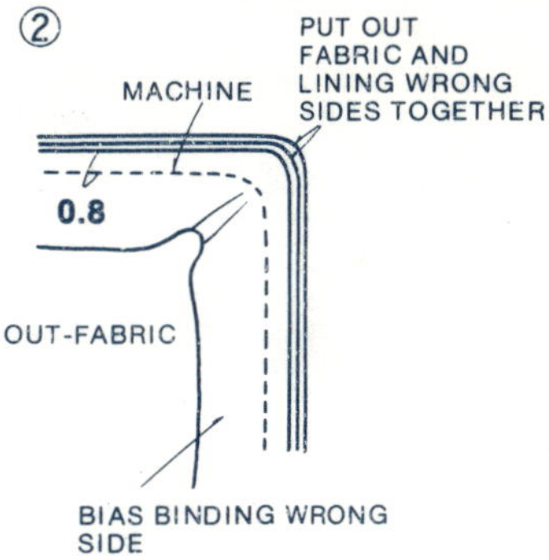

②
MACHINE
PUT OUT FABRIC AND LINING WRONG SIDES TOGETHER
0.8
OUT-FABRIC
BIAS BINDING WRONG SIDE

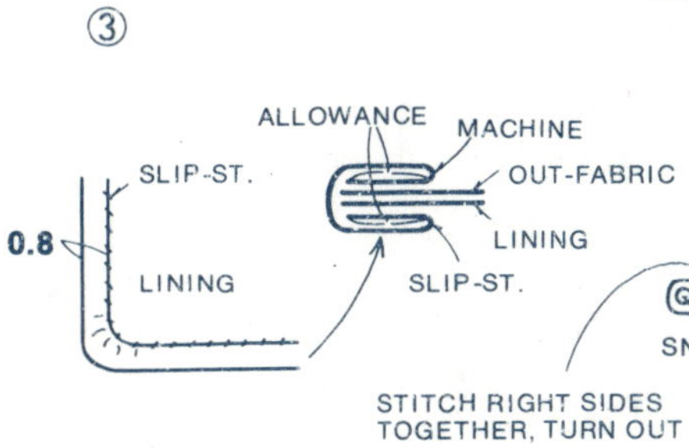

③
ALLOWANCE
MACHINE
SLIP-ST.
OUT-FABRIC
LINING
0.8
LINING
SLIP-ST.
STITCH RIGHT SIDES TOGETHER, TURN OUT

FINISHED DIAGRAM:

SNAPS
18 cm
6.5 cm

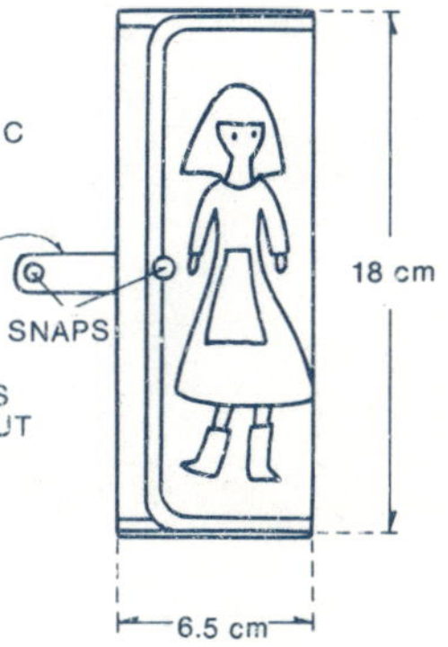

✲ SCHOOL BAG Shown on page 71. ✲

***You'll Need:**

80 cm by 40 cm each of Pink cotton heavy weight, stripe with flowers against White cotton. Felt; 8 cm by 6 cm White, 3 cm square Light Brown.

***Finished Size:** Refer to diagram.

***Making Instructions:**

Cut pieces as shown, cut felt for applique following to design.

Work applique and embroidery on out fabric where indicated, make bag following to ①–③.

CUTTING: CUT 1 OUT-FABRIC PINK COTTON, CUT LINING STRIPE WITH FLOWERS AGAINST WHITE COTTON

1 TURNING
EMBROIDERY POSITION
60
1 ALLOWANCE
M
6
FOLD
36

HAND-BELT, CUT 2 PINK COTTON

1
1 ALLOWANCE
8
32

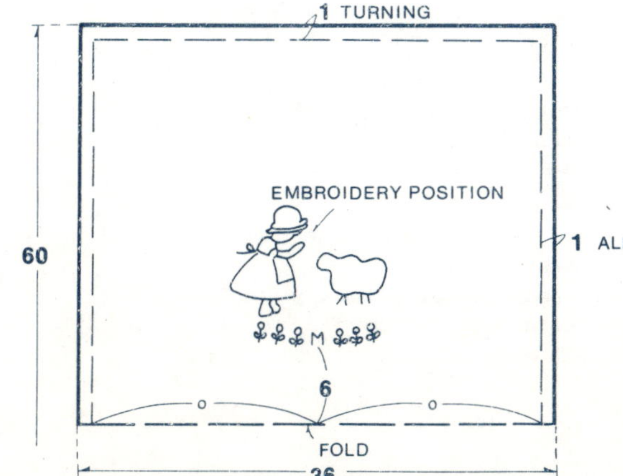

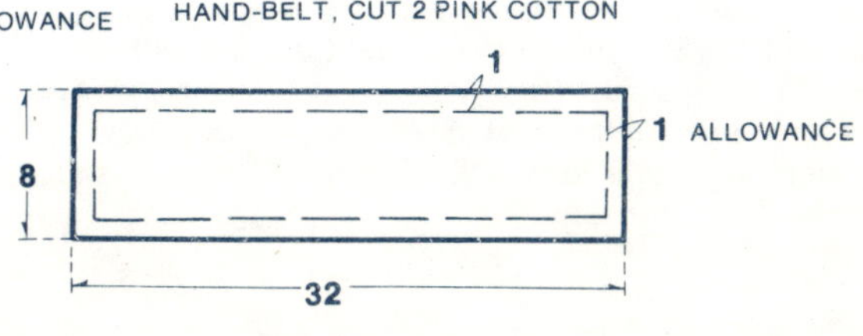

PATTERN (ACTUAL SIZE); 3 STRANDS UNLESS SPECIFIED.

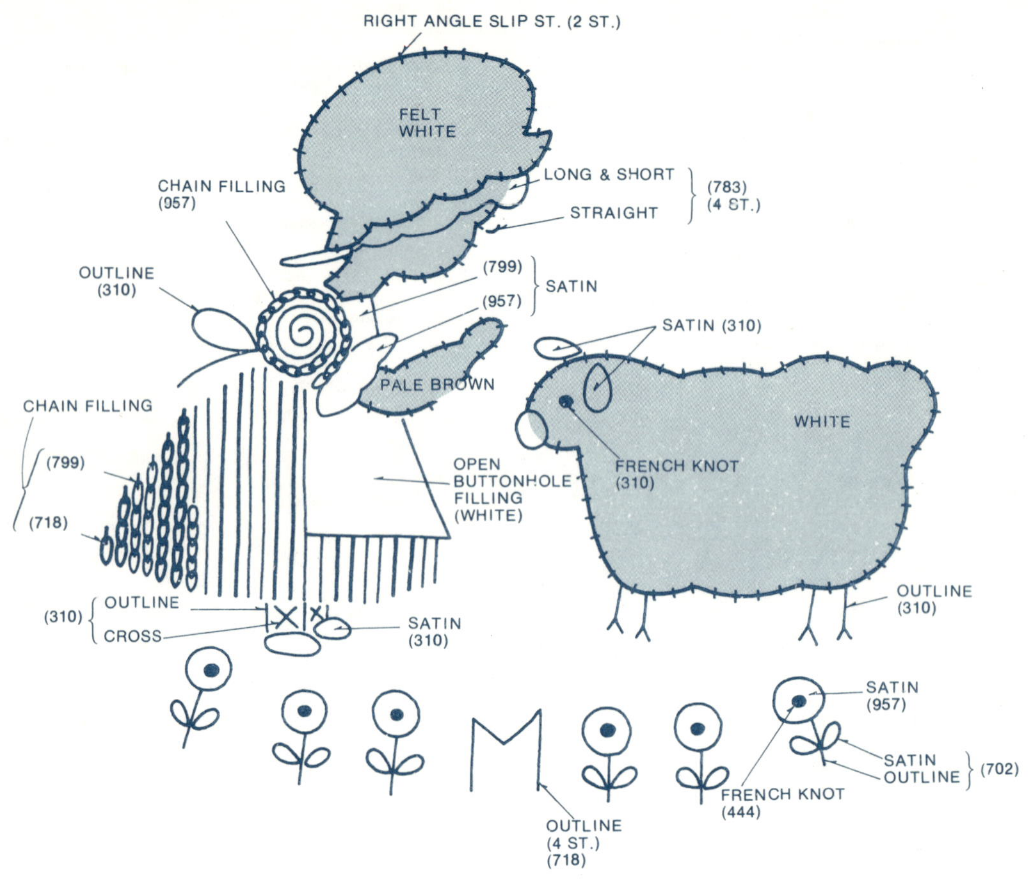

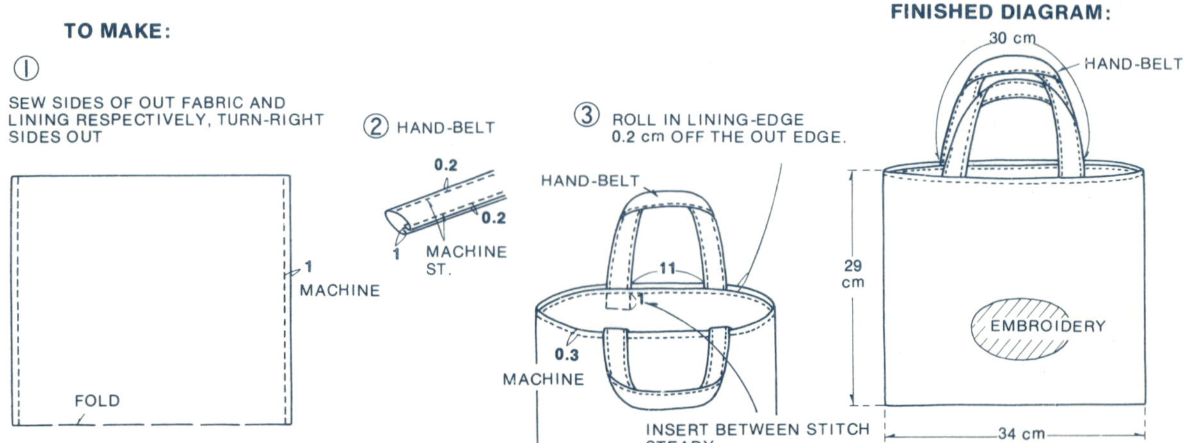

✲ ABACUS CASE Shown on page 70. ✲

***You'll Need:**

60 cm by 30 cm Yellow cotton fabric. 4 cm by 3 cm Red felt. D.M.C. Stranded Cotton: small amount each of 519 (Sky Blue), 946 (Fire Red), 741 (Tangerine Yellow). 703 (Brilliant Green), White, 433 (Umber), 899 (Soft Pink), 3689 (Raspberry Red), 817 (Geranium Red), 208 (Parma Violet), 310 (Black).

***Finished Size:** Refer to diagram.

***Making Instructions:**

Cut fabric pieces as shown, cut felt for applique following to design.

Work embroidery and applique where indicated, make abacus case following to ①–④.

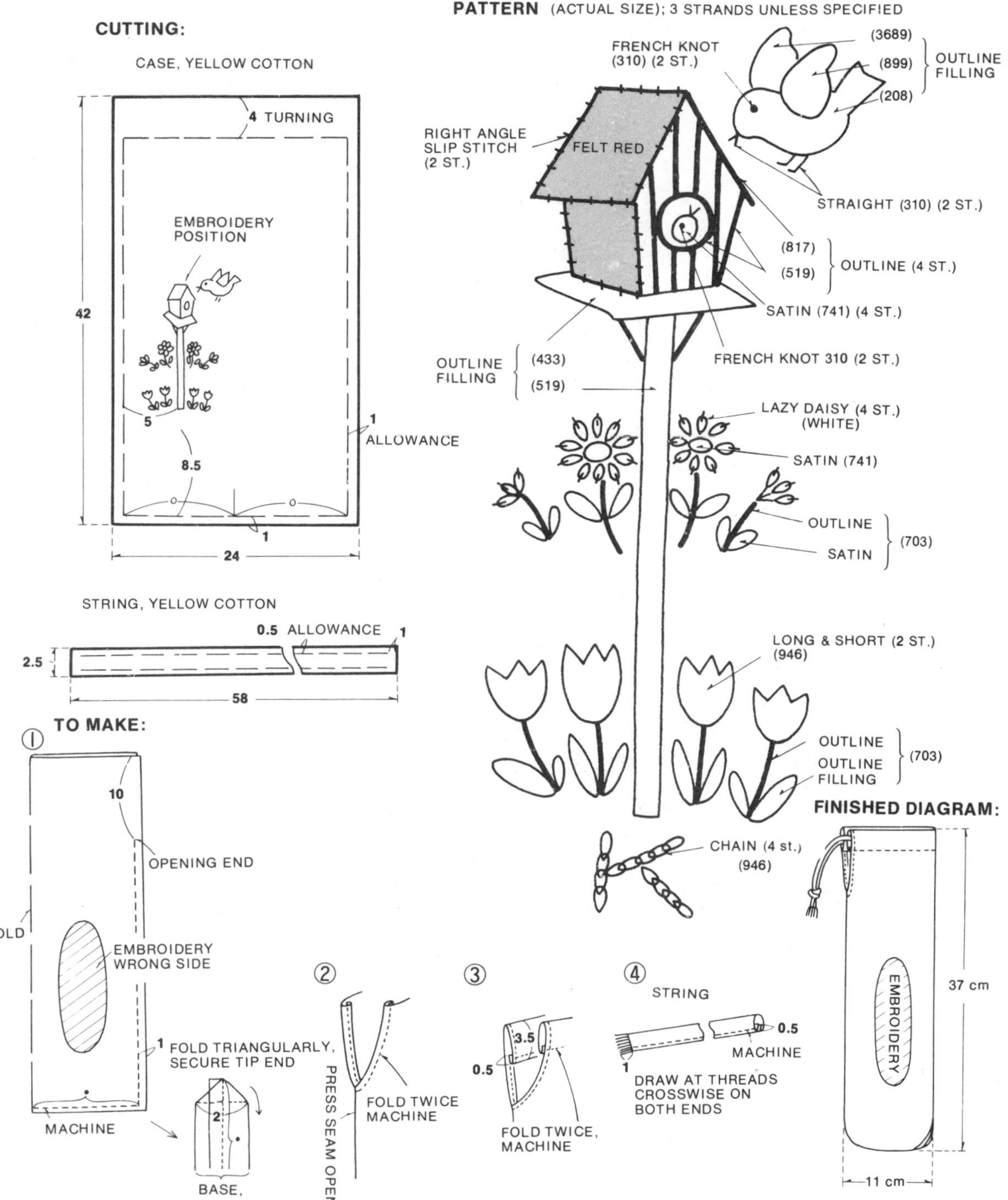

✲ SACK FOR EXERCISE WEAR Shown on page 70. ✲

You'll Need:

80 cm by 35 cm Blue soft denim. Felt; 20 cm by 10 cm Light Brown, 15 cm by 7 cm White, 7 cm square Dark Brown, 8 cm by 6 cm each of Gold Yellow, Black, 7 cm by 5 cm each of Blue, Fire Red. D.M.C. Stranded Cotton: small amount each of 444 (Buttercup Yellow), 946 (Fire Red), 912 (Emerald Green), 310 (Black), Felt color.

***Finished Size:** Refer to diagram.

***Making Instructions:**

Cut fabric pieces as shown, cut felt for applique following to design.

Having appliqued on the position indicated, work emboidery, make into sack following to ①–④. Pass strings through as shown.

PATTERN (ACTUAL SIZE)
DARK BROWN
OUTLINE (4 ST.)
(444)
PALE
BROWN
BLACK
OUTLINE (3 st.)
(946)
SATIN (3 ST.)
(310)
GOLD YELLOW
PALE
BROWN
PALE BROWN
PALE BROWN
OUTLINE (4 ST.)
(912)
WHITE
WHITE
BLUE
FIRE RED
FOLD
RIGHT ANGLE
SLIP STITCH
(2 ST.)
FOLD
PALE
BROWN
PALE BROWN
WHITE
WHITE

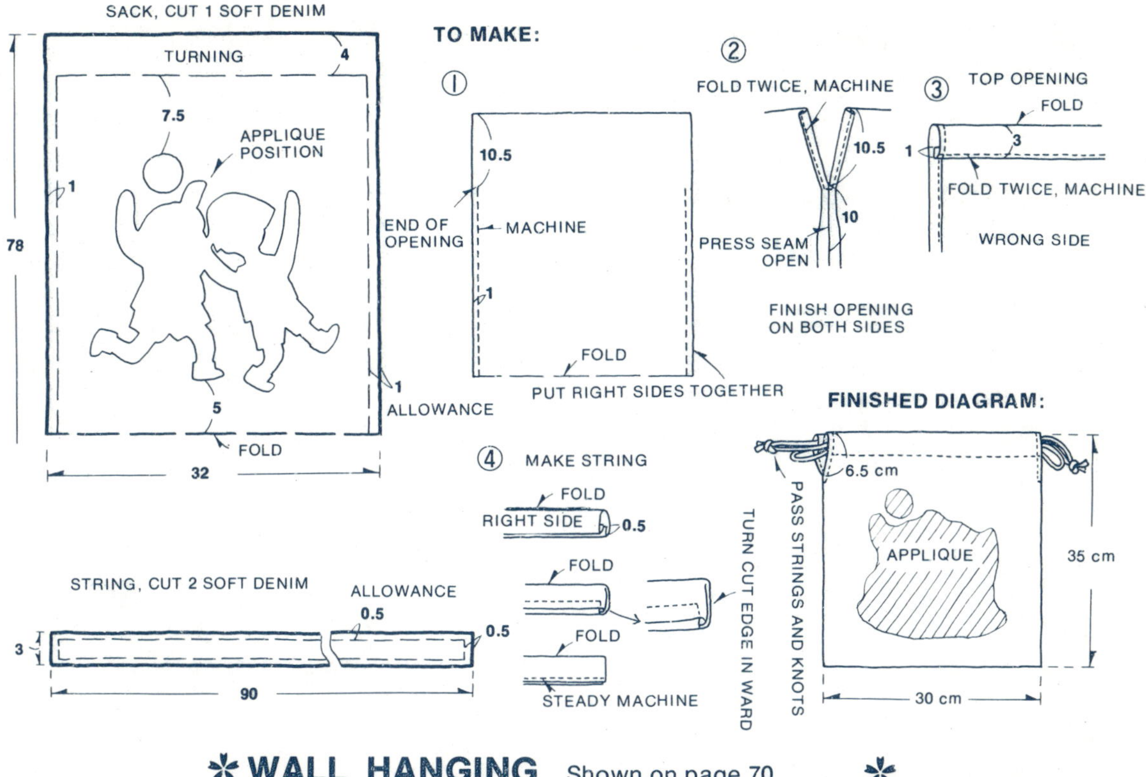

✲ WALL HANGING Shown on page 70. ✲

***You'll Need:**

90 cm by 40 cm Dark Blue heavy weight cotton. 250 cm of 1.5 cm cotton tape Red. Felt; 12 cm by 10 cm each of White, Blue, 14 cm by 7 cm Deep Pink, 12 cm by 8 cm Orange, 9 cm square Yellow, 8 cm by 7 cm Pale Cream, 7 cm square Pale Pink, 9 cm by 3 cm each of Cream, Light Blue, 6 cm by 5 cm Fire Red, 4 cm by 3 cm Pale Blue, small amount of Yellow Green. D.M.C. Stranded Cotton: small amount each of 603 (Cerise), Felt color.

CHART ON MEASUREMENTS:

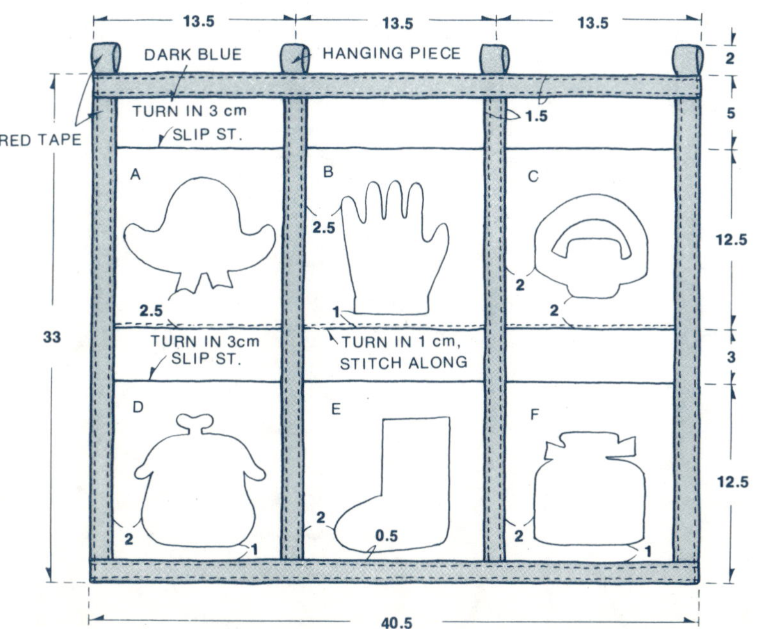

***Finished Size:**

Refer to diagram.

***Making Instructions:**

Cut 1 of background, 2 of pocket from fabric with seam allowance, cut felt for applique following to design.

Turn in top edge of pocket 3 cm, slip stitch steady, work applique on the position indicated with right angle slip-stitch.

Lay pockets and tape on the background piece as shown, machine stitch all around putting hanging pieces below the tape on top.

PATTERN (ACTUAL SIZE)

*BAG Shown on page 72. *

***You'll Need:**

70 cm by 75 cm Dark Blue denim. 70 cm by 60 cm Red and White gingham cheek. D.M.C. Stranded Cotton: 1 skein each of 666 (Poppy), White; small amount of 702 (Brilliant Green), 310 (Black).

***Finished Size:** Refer to diagram.

***Making Instructions:**

Cut fabric referring to the chart of cutting, work embroidery on the pocket where indicated.

Sew into bag following to ①–③.

PATTERN (ACTUAL SIZE)

3 STRANDS UNLESS SPECIFIED
OUTLINE (666)
LAZY DAISY
STRAIGHT (4 ST.) (702)
SATIN (WHITE)
FRENCH KNOT (WHITE)
(666)
(WHITE)
OUTLINE FILLING
(WHITE)
(310)
SATIN

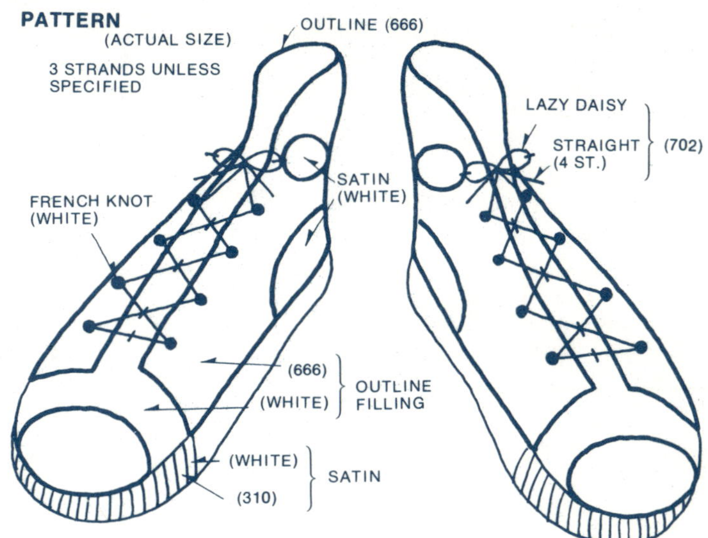

CUTTING:

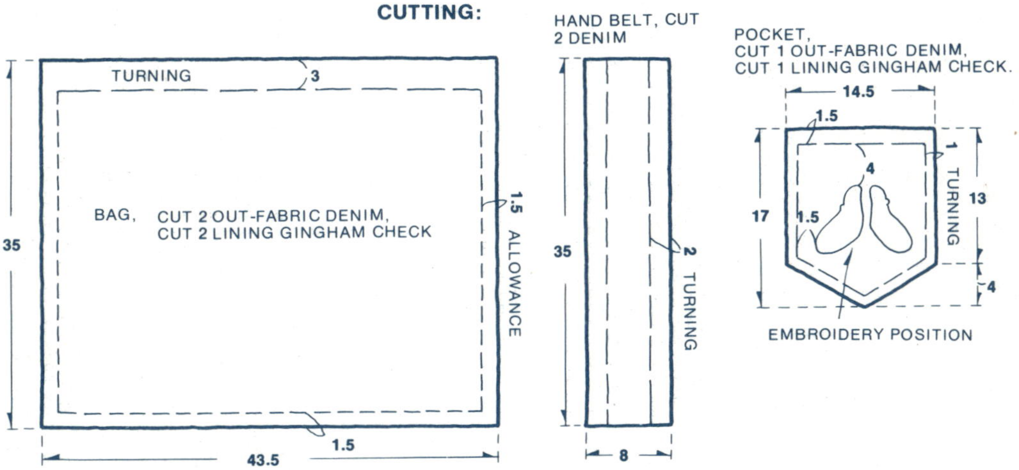

TURNING
3
BAG, CUT 2 OUT-FABRIC DENIM, CUT 2 LINING GINGHAM CHECK
1.5 ALLOWANCE
35
1.5
43.5
HAND BELT, CUT 2 DENIM
35
2 TURNING
8
POCKET, CUT 1 OUT-FABRIC DENIM, CUT 1 LINING GINGHAM CHECK.
14.5
1.5
4
1.5
17
1 TURNING
13
4
EMBROIDERY POSITION

TO MAKE:

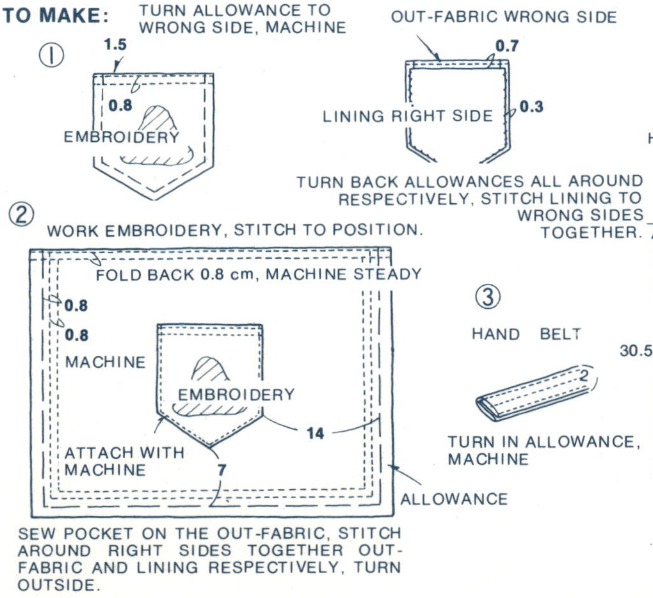

①
TURN ALLOWANCE TO WRONG SIDE, MACHINE
1.5
0.8
EMBROIDERY
OUT-FABRIC WRONG SIDE
0.7
LINING RIGHT SIDE
0.3
TURN BACK ALLOWANCES ALL AROUND RESPECTIVELY, STITCH LINING TO WRONG SIDES TOGETHER.
②
WORK EMBROIDERY, STITCH TO POSITION.
FOLD BACK 0.8 cm, MACHINE STEADY
0.8
0.8
MACHINE
EMBROIDERY
14
ATTACH WITH MACHINE
7
ALLOWANCE
SEW POCKET ON THE OUT-FABRIC, STITCH AROUND RIGHT SIDES TOGETHER OUT-FABRIC AND LINING RESPECTIVELY, TURN OUTSIDE.
③
HAND BELT
2
TURN IN ALLOWANCE, MACHINE

FINISHED DIAGRAM:

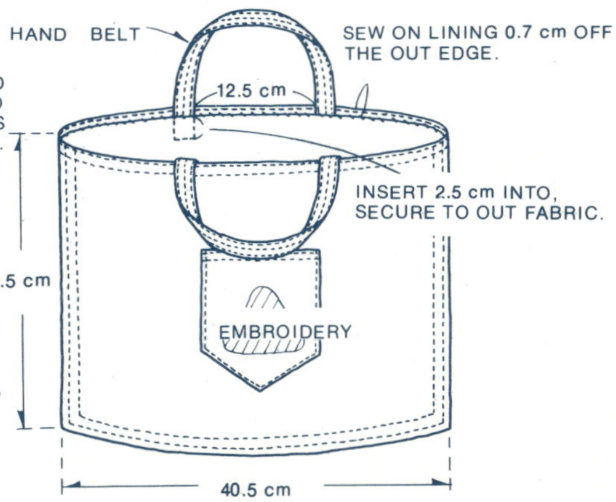

HAND BELT
SEW ON LINING 0.7 cm OFF THE OUT EDGE.
12.5 cm
INSERT 2.5 cm INTO, SECURE TO OUT FABRIC.
30.5 cm
EMBROIDERY
40.5 cm

✻VANITY CASE Shown on page 72. ✻

***You'll Need:**

45 cm by 25 cm each of Yellow Green cotton, Yellow Green and White checked gingham. D.M.C. Stranded Cotton: Small amount each of 743 (Tangerine Yellow), 946 (Fire Red), 310 (Black). 20 cm long zip-fastener.

***Finished Size:** Refer to diagram.

***Making Instructions:**

Cut pieces out from fabric referring to the chart of cutting, copy design on out piece referring to ① for its position, work embroidery.

Make following to ①–③.

PATTERN (ACTUAL SIZE) 3 STRANDS

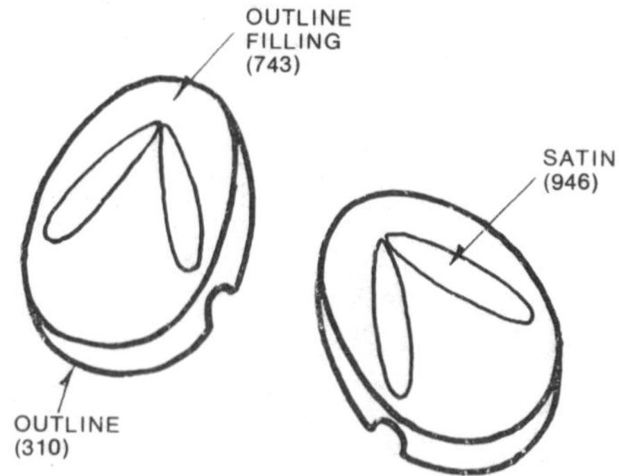

TO MAKE:

CUTTING:

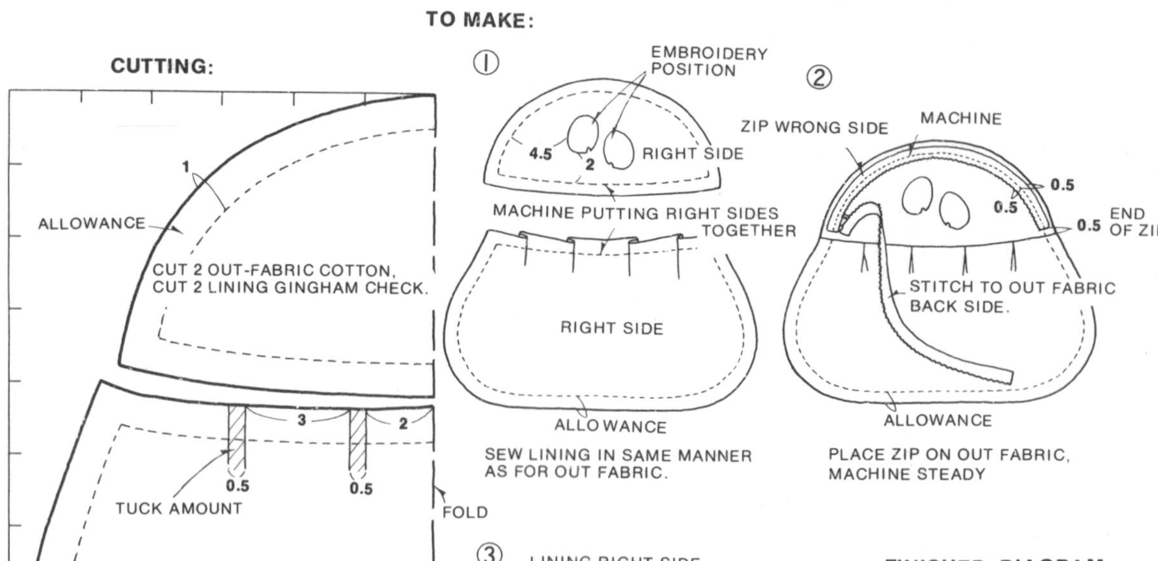

CUT 2 OUT-FABRIC COTTON,
CUT 2 LINING GINGHAM CHECK.

1

2 cm ALLOWANCE

2 cm

③ LINING RIGHT SIDE

TURN IN LINING EDGE, SEW ON ZIP TAPE.

FINISHED DIAGRAM:

18 cm

21 cm

✱ CUSHION Shown on page 72. ✱

***You'll Need:**

70 cm by 40 cm Cherry Pink velvet. D.M.C. Stranded Cotton: small amount each of 3350 & 3354 (Old Rose), 905 (Parakeet Green), 3348 (Scarab Green), Gold, Silver. 100 grams kapok.

***Finished Size:** Refer to diagram.

***Making Instructions:**

Cut fabric following to pattern, work embroidery front side where indicated. Stitch out edge putting right sides together, turn out side, stuff kapok, stitch opening closed.

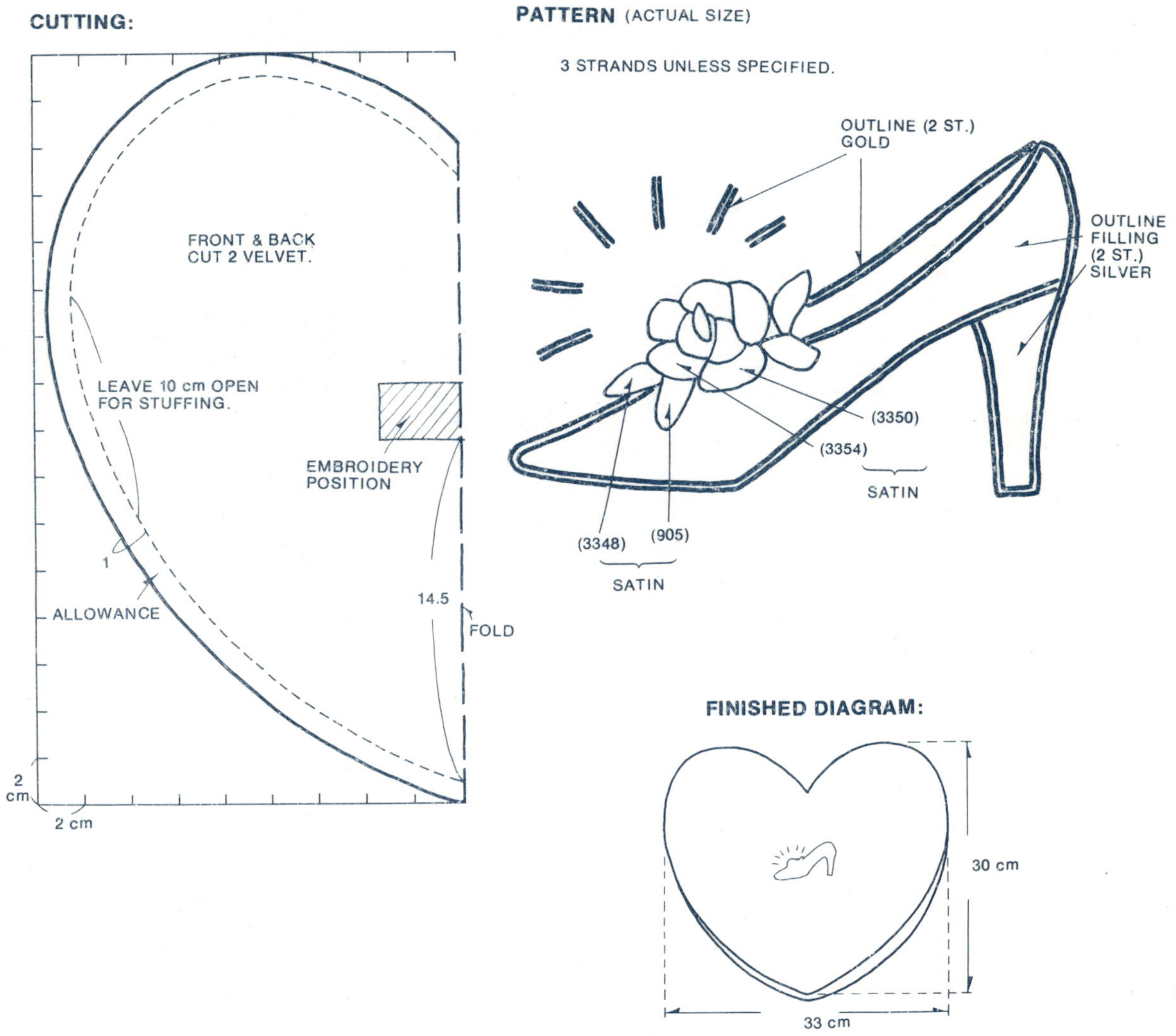

EMBROIDERY STITCHES

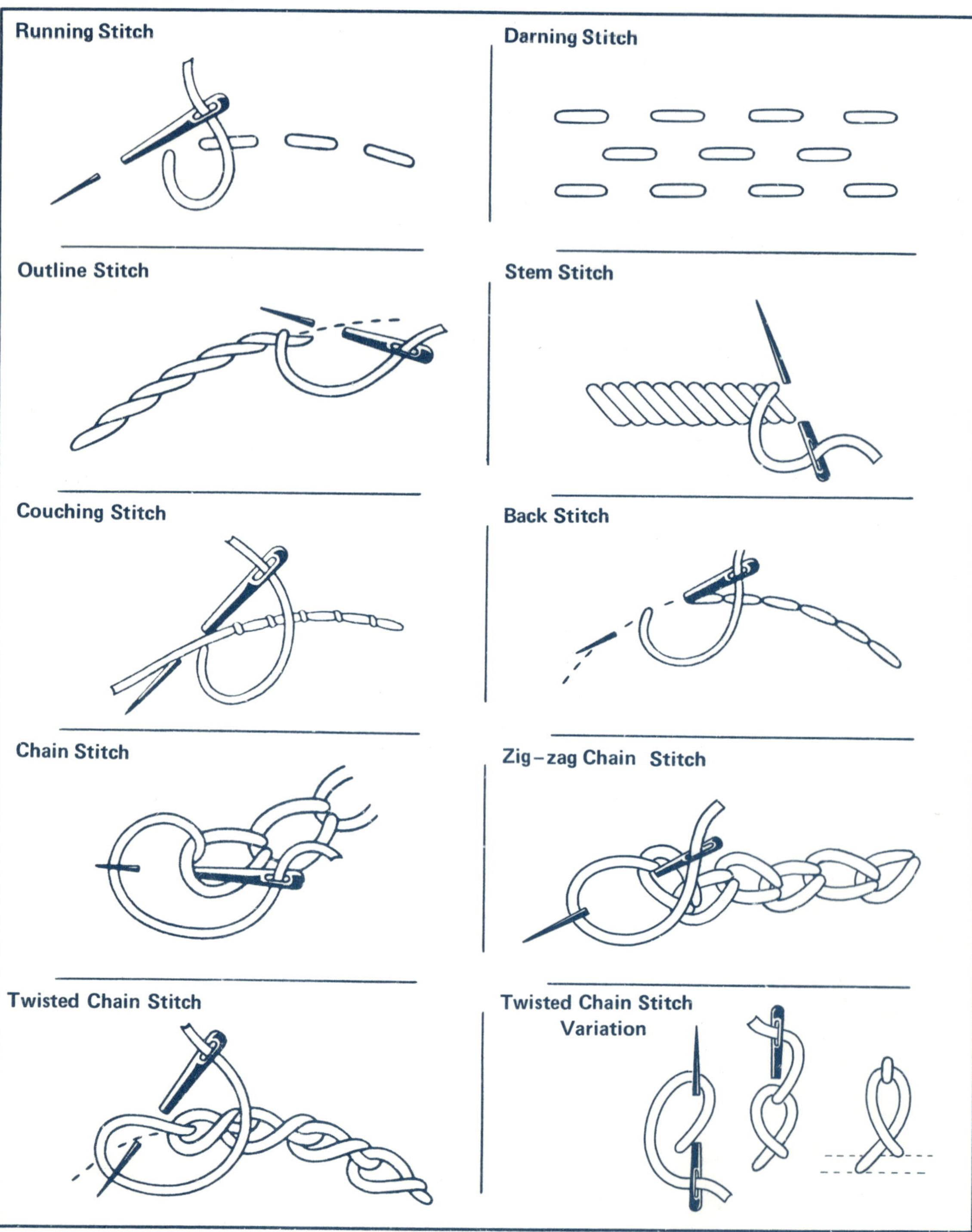

Cable Chain Stitch

Zig zag Stitch

Herringbone Stitch

Lazy Daisy Stitch

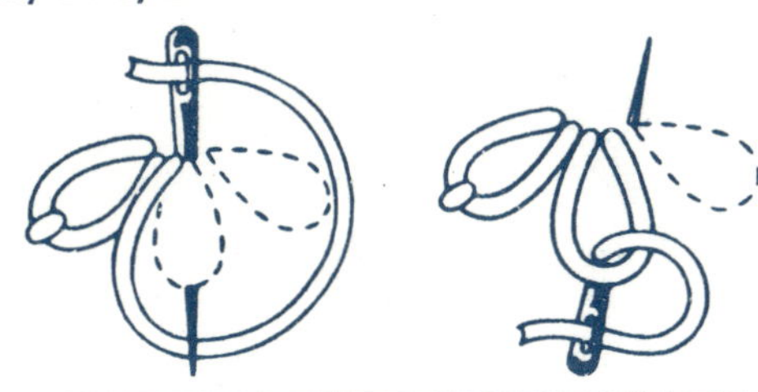

Open Buttonhole stitch

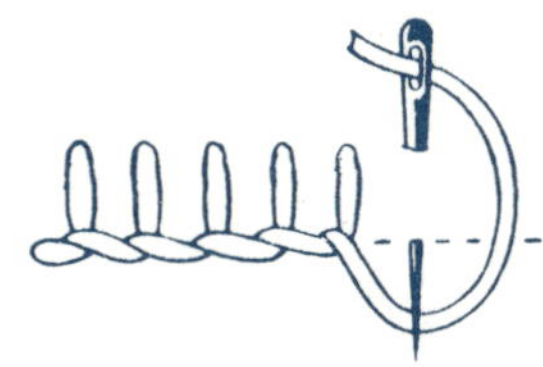

Buttonhole Filling Stitch

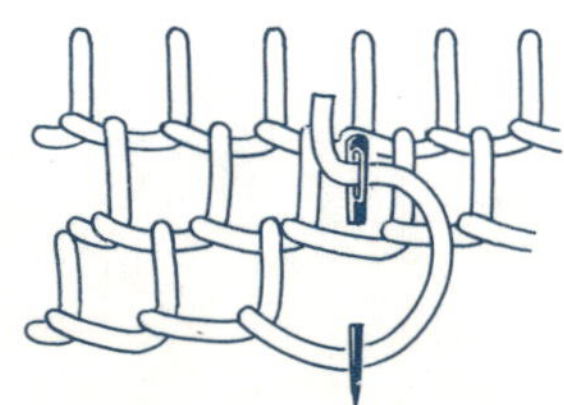

Single Knot Stitch

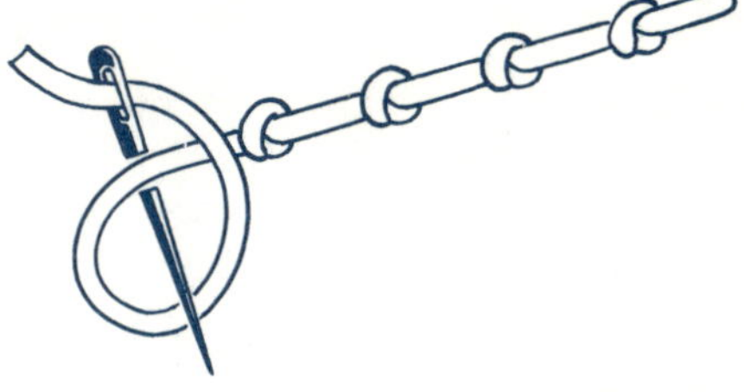

Straight Stitch

Closed Herringbone Stitch

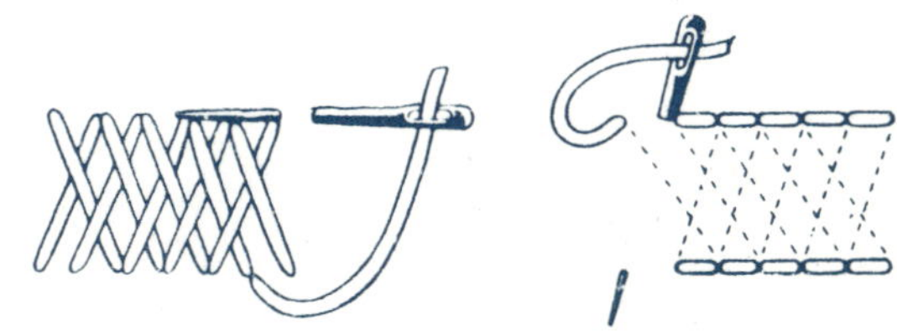

Double Lazy Daisy Stitch

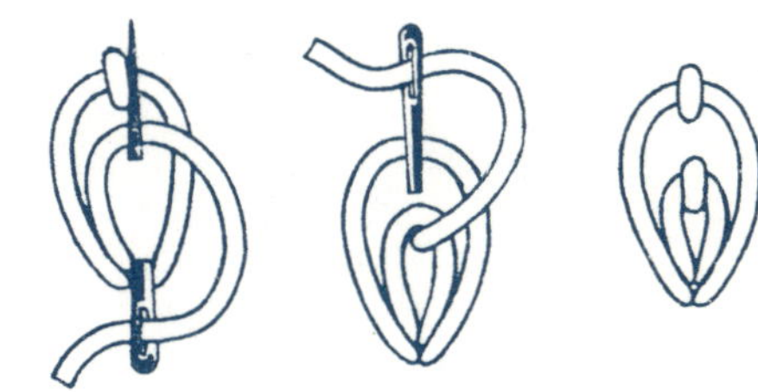

Closed Buttonhole Stitch

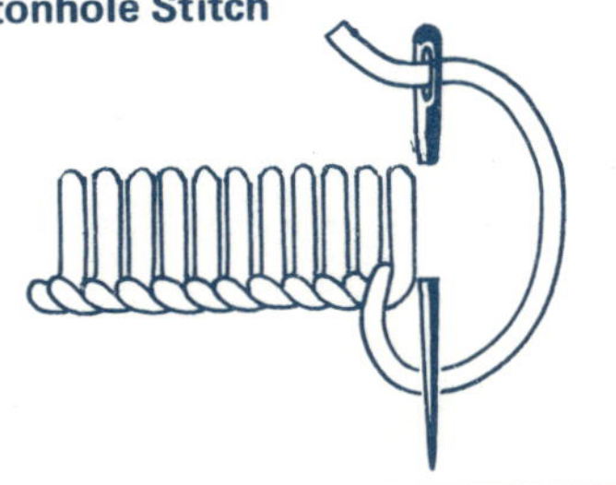

Couched Trellis Stitch

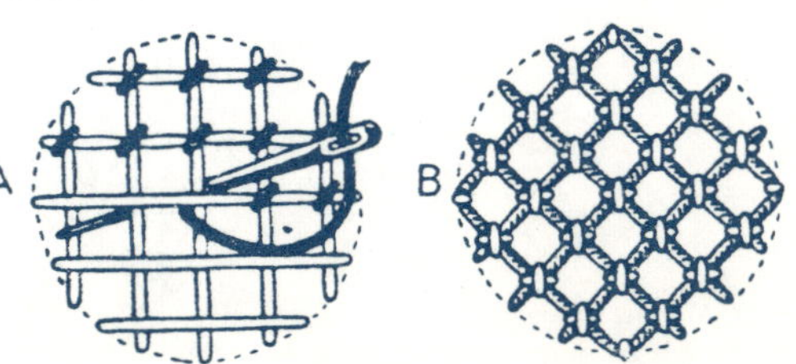

French Knot Stitch

French Knot Filling Stitch

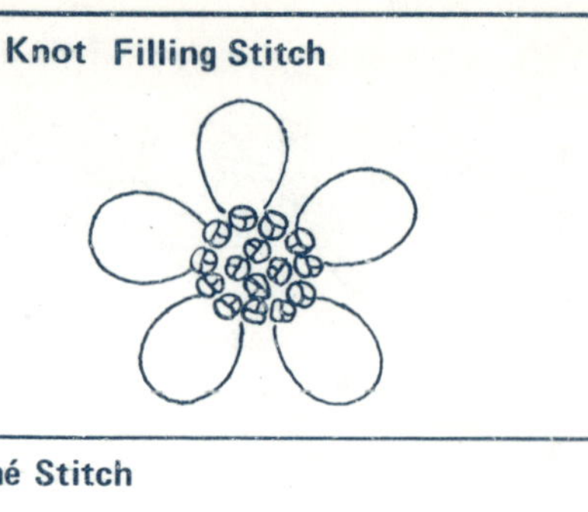

German Knot Stitch

Macramé Stitch

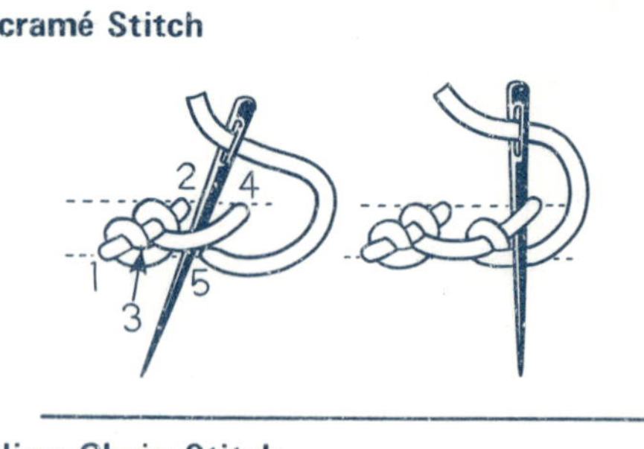

Bullion Stitch

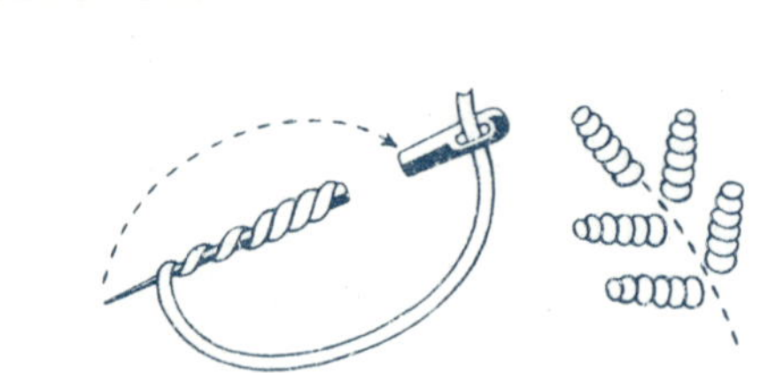

Bullion Chain Stitch

Bullion Knot Stitch

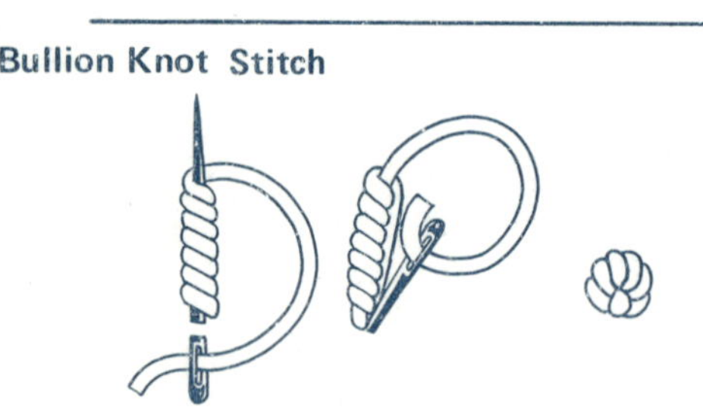

Fly Stitch

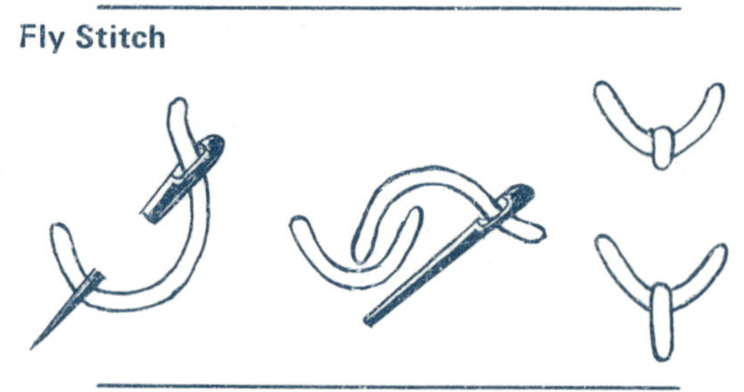

Fern Stitch

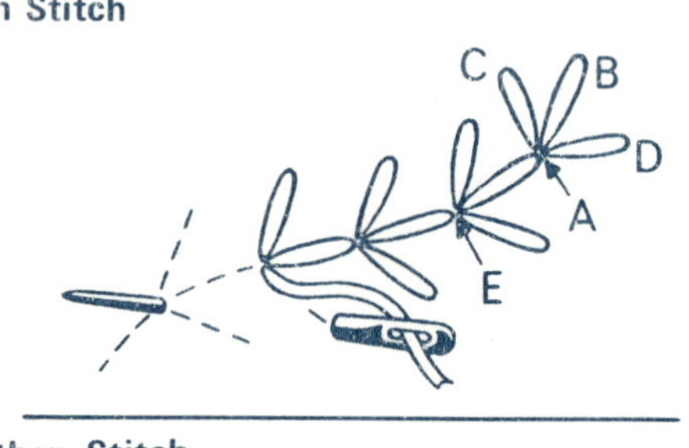

Fern Stitch Variation

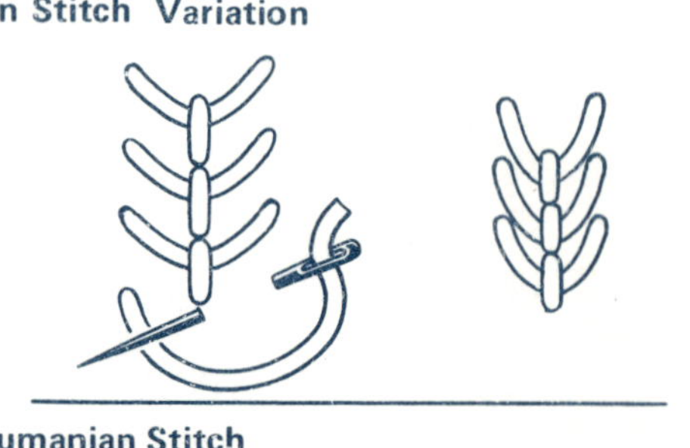

Feather Stitch

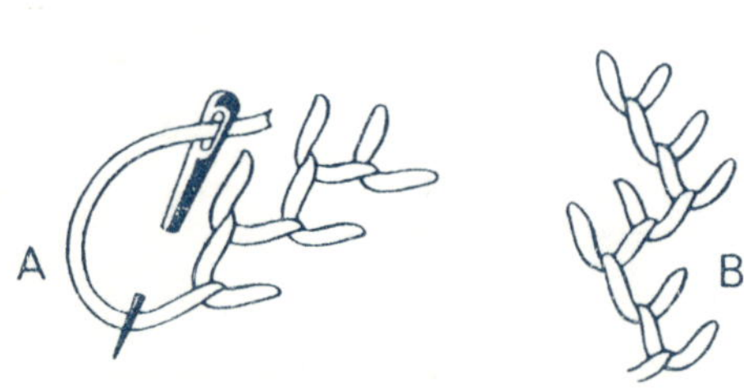

Roumanian Stitch

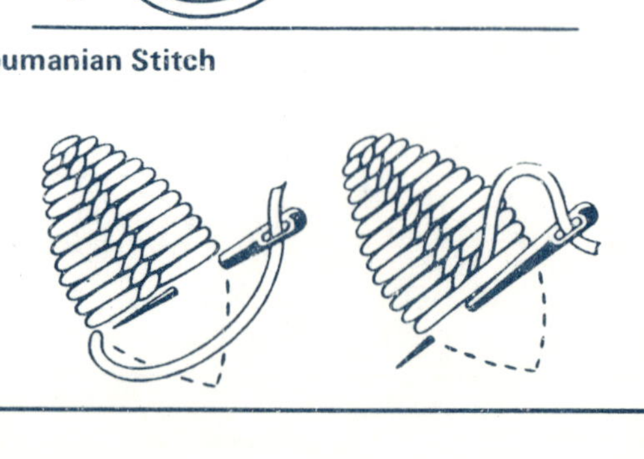

Leaf Stitch

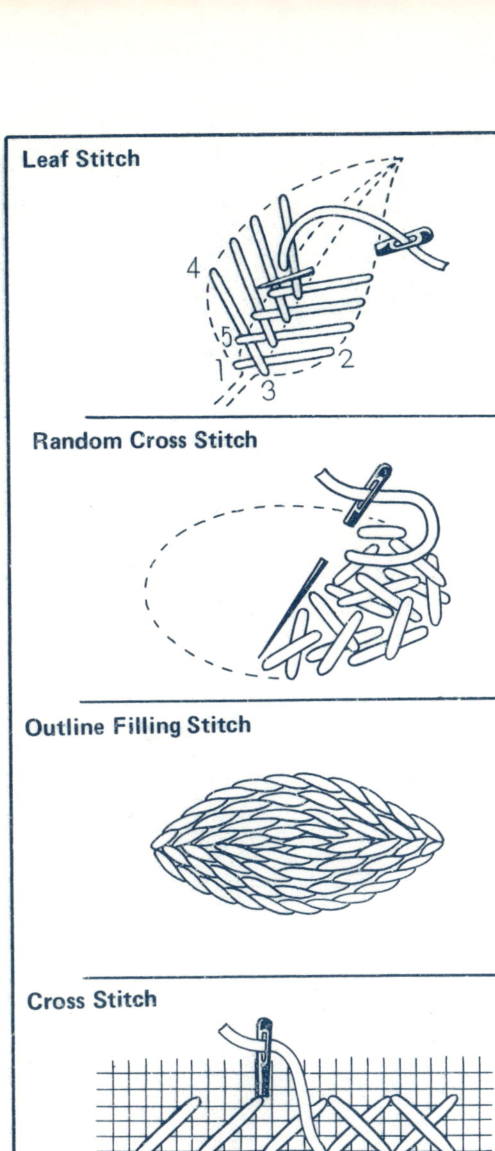

Random Cross Stitch

Outline Filling Stitch

Cross Stitch

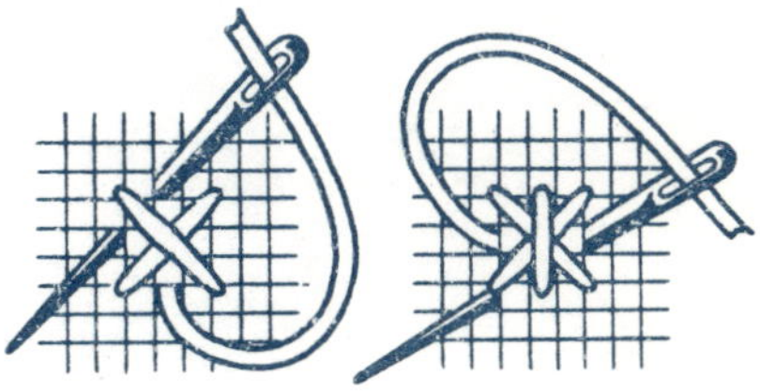

Whipped Running Stitch

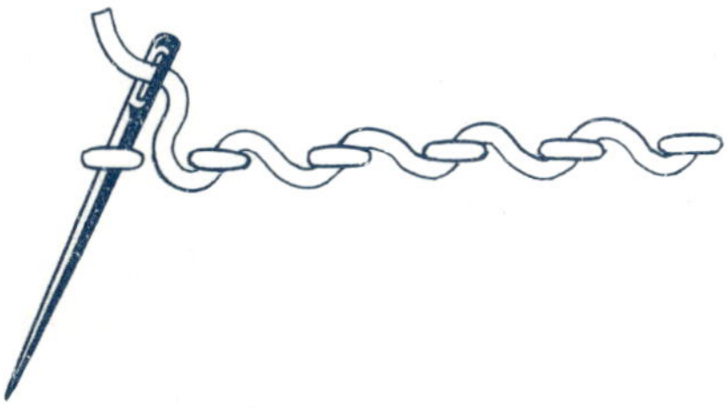

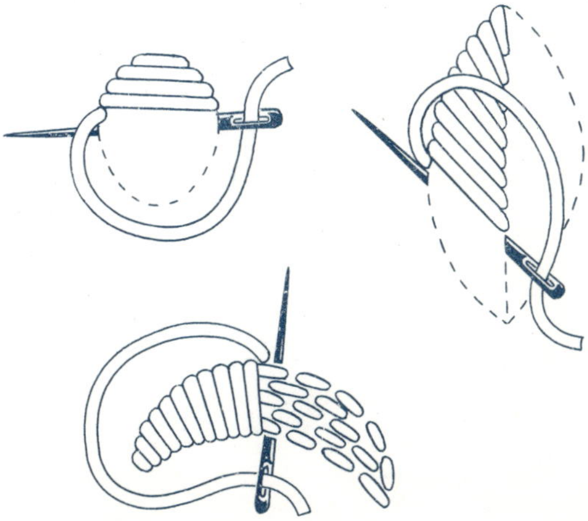

Whipped Chain Stitch

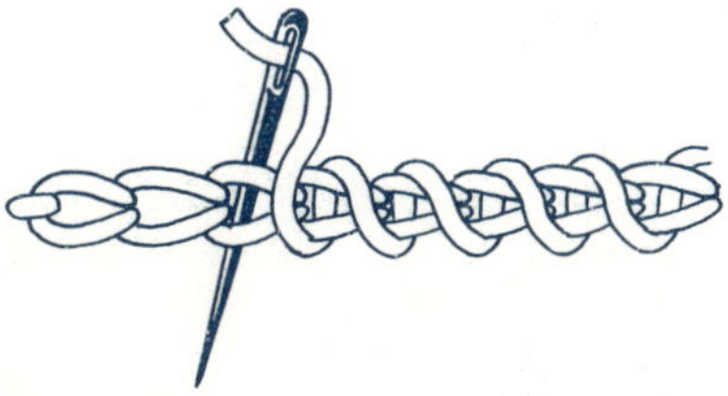

Fishbone Stitch

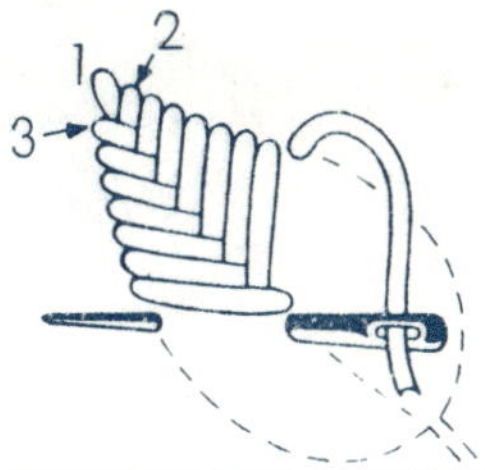

Seed Filling Stitch

Chain Filling Stitch

Double Cross Stitch

Satin Stitch

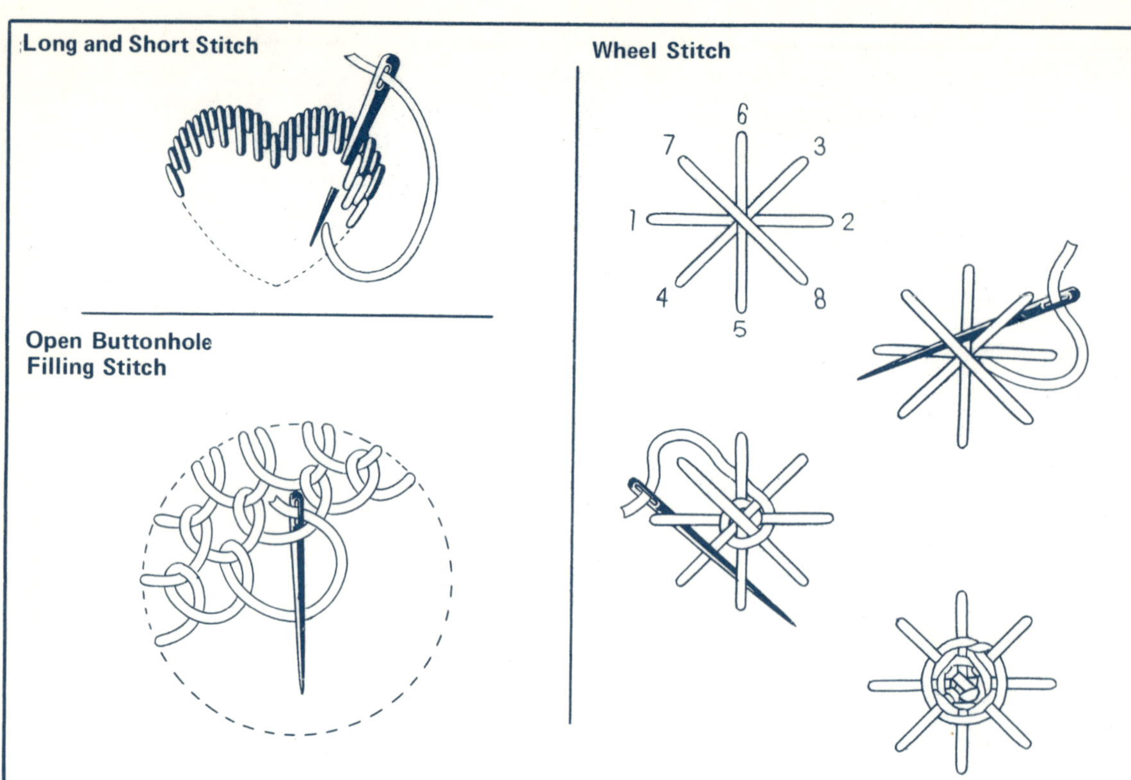

The way to Applique

When you are ready to work applique, copy design on the back-ground fabric, glue applique fabric to its position or tack along the edge to steady, then begin to work applique.

Chain Stitch

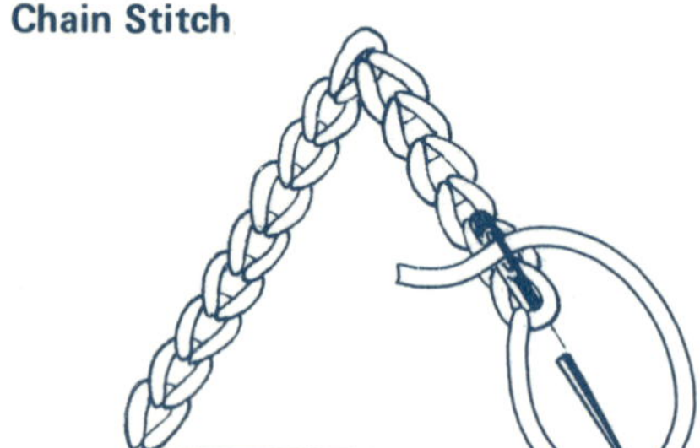

Steady applique fabric trimming along the edge with chain stitch.

Open Buttonhole Stitch

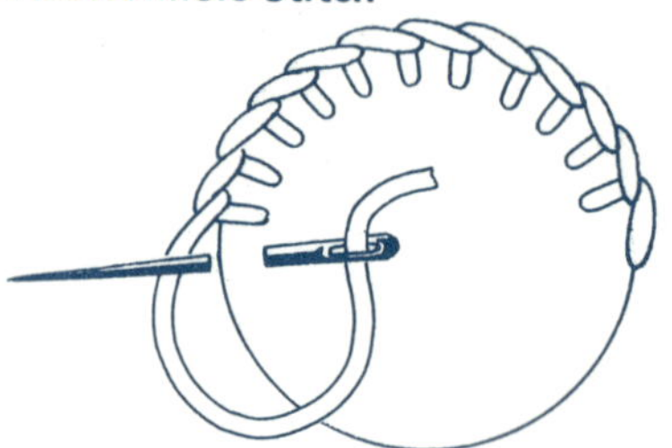

This stitch is commonly used to work on the piece with no allowance.

Outline Stitch

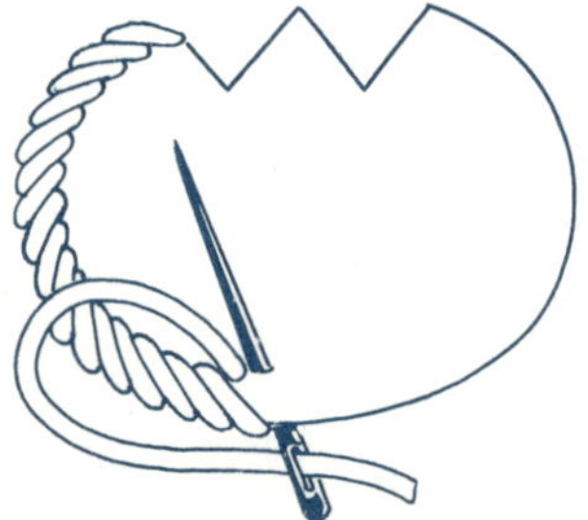

Steady applique fabric trimming along the edge with outline stitch.

Right-Angled Slip Stitch

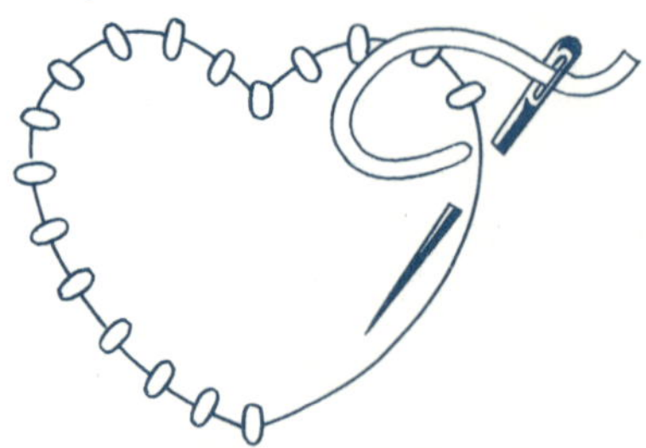

This stitch is also used to form invisible stitches making each stitch right angle to the outline of applique fabric. Stitches are sometimes worked out roughly with contrasting thread to give the work an accent.

EMBROIDERY THREADS

THE MOST POPULAR FOR EMBROIDERY ARE No.25 and No.5.

No.25—One thread consists of 6 strands, and measures 8m per skein. You can pull out as many threads as required from the bundle if necessary (according to the design).

No.5—Single thick thread, and is quite lustrous. One skein measures 25m. Suitable for rough stitches.

Besides these, you have a wide variety of them such as cottons, rayons, silk, wools . . . even metal threads. The sizes also range from thick, medium, fine and extreme fine.

HANDLING THE THREAD

The threads Nos. 25, 5 and 4 come in a bundle or ring, depending on the manufacturer. When they are formed in a ring, untie the twist, and cut one end of the ring with scissors, and pull out one by one. When they are gathered together and held by one or two paper labels, pull out the length from the core of the bundle.

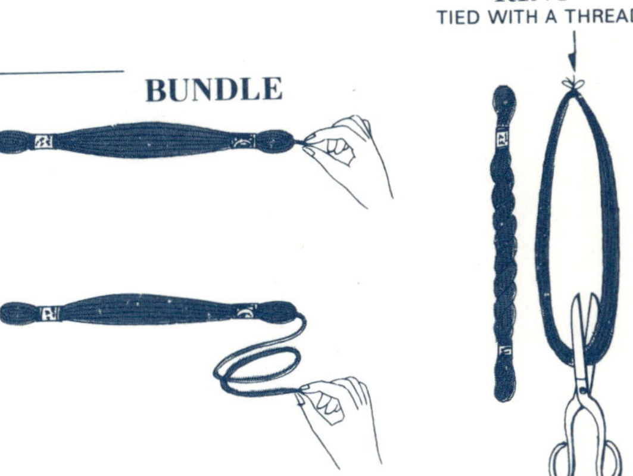

PASSING THE THREAD THROUGH THE NEEDLE

When you pass 4 strands of the thread through an embroidery needle, fold the ends of the threads, and insert the folded edge through hole of the needle. (See illustration on right) Do the same way when you pass a thick yarn like wool.

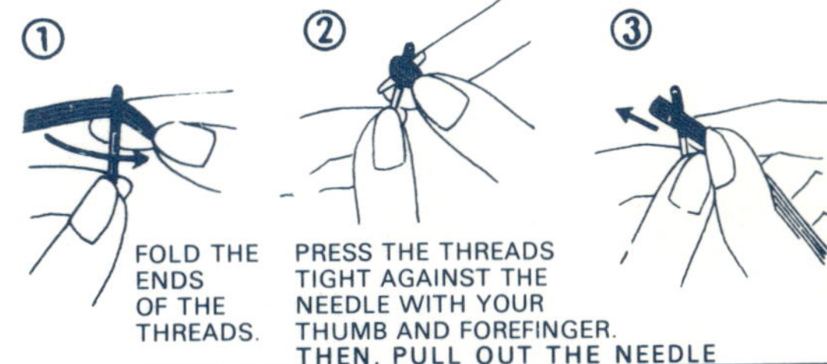

FOLD THE ENDS OF THE THREADS.

PRESS THE THREADS TIGHT AGAINST THE NEEDLE WITH YOUR THUMB AND FOREFINGER. THEN, PULL OUT THE NEEDLE

HINTS ON STITCHING

HOW TO START AND END STITCHING

A securing knot is rarely made in embroidery. To start stitching, see the illustration below. If you need to make a knot, form a small loop round the needle, and gently pull out the needle, with your left thumb pressing the loop.

GENERAL STITCHING

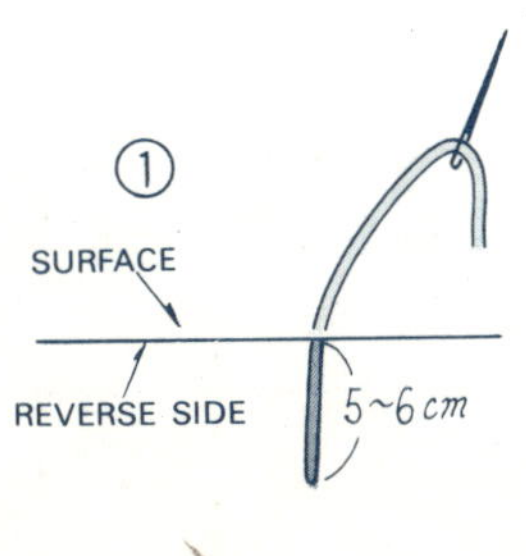

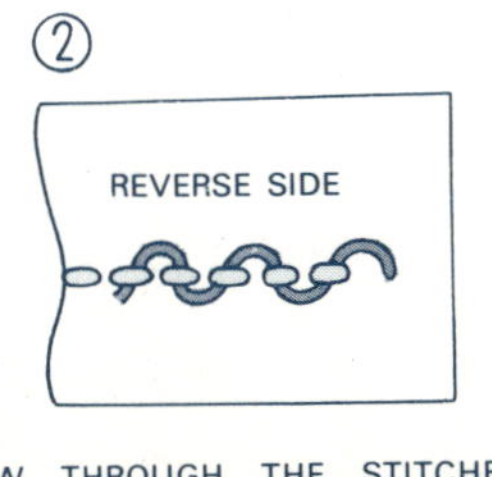

SEW THROUGH THE STITCHES ON THE REVERSE SIDE (NOT SHOWING ON THE SURFACE WHEN STARTING OR ENDING THE SEAM.

FILLING STITCHING

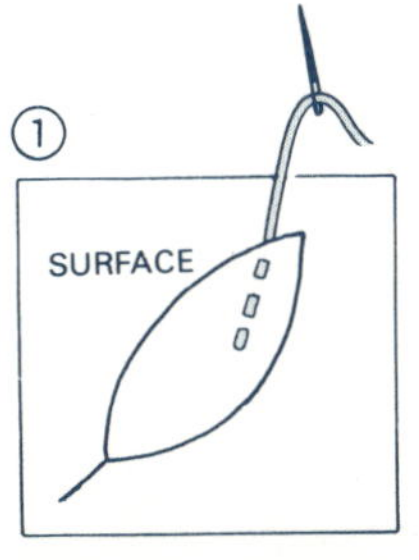

SEW A FEW STITCHES TOWARD THE STARTING POINT.

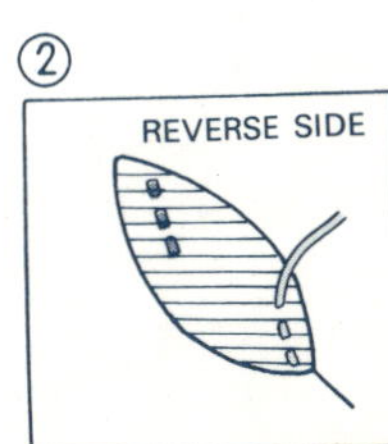

SEW BACK A FEW STITCHES BEFORE BREAKING OFF (CAREFULLY NOT TO SHOW THE SEAM ON FRONT).

HOW TO TRANSFER A DESIGN

Place a sheet of thin paper over the design, and copy it drawing with a hard (lead) pencil.

USING TRACING PAPER

Place the waxed side of the tracing paper which is produced for dressmaking, down on the right side of the material that's been pinned on a board. Put the thin paper, with design over the tracing paper, and work round carefully with a steel pen or a hard pencil, or a tracing wheel.

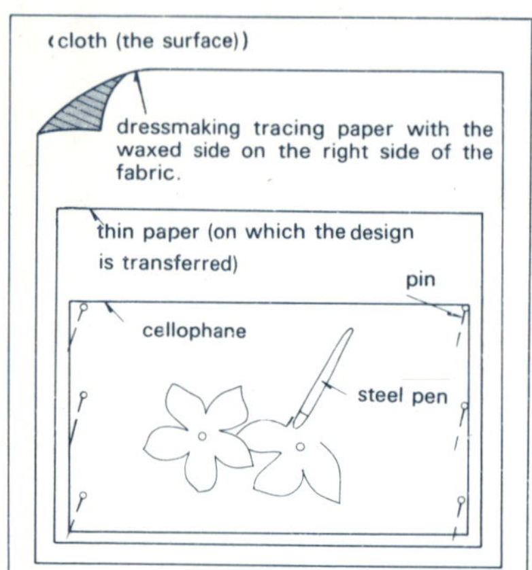

USING A GLASS PLATE

Bridge two boxes with a piece of opaque glass (to minimize eyestrain) and put a lighted bulb under the glass. Transfer a design found in book onto thin paper. Then put the paper on the glass, lay the material on it and outline directly on the material with a hard pencil.

USING TISSUE PAPER

Trace the design onto a sheet of smooth tissue paper, and tack this into position at the edges of the background material. Using a basting thread, tack around the whole of the design through the tissue paper and material. Embroider over it, then remove the paper.

ENLARGING THE DESIGN

Draw a graph with right squares over the design. The more complicated the design, the smaller the squares. Then draw in another piece of paper the squares that are enlarged at regular rate, and trace the design in the enlarged graph. Do the opposite when reducing the design.